JARGON 101

"This is it. I believe this is sholy it. Yep. This is *good*." — Roy Blount, Jr.

"What fun! This book makes you want to spit in yer skillet and start cookin' vittles!" — Judith Olney (author of *Joy of Chocolate, Summer Food, and Judith Olney's Entertainments*)

"WHITE TRASH COOKING is (dare I say it?) a gas! And coming from the founder of the White Trash Liberation Movement, that's a real compliment!" — Ed McClanahan (author of *The Natural Man* and *Famous People I Have Known*)

"Looking through it, it's clear to me what I am!" — James B. Hunt, Jr., Former Governor of North Carolina

"I'd stop and eat in any of these kitchens, rather than Colonel Sanders or Chez Panisse, for the talk alone." — Ronald Johnson (author of *The American Table, Southwestern Cooking,* and *The Uncookbook*)

"WHITE TRASH COOKING is wonderful. The photographs are a brilliant addition to the recipes. It is the funniest book I have seen in years." — Mark Holburn, Editor, *Aperture*

SPONSOR TO THE EDITION

CHARLOTTE & PHILIP HANES *(Winston-Salem)*

"She don't know me from Adam's housecat."
— Nelda Welch, Hot Coffee, Mississippi

WHITE TRASH COOKING

Ernest Matthew Mickler

With Color Photographs by the Author

THE JARGON SOCIETY

Second Printing (April, 1986)

Library of Congress Catalog Card Number: 85-080302
ISBN: 0-912330-59-7

Design by Jonathan Greene

Decorative cover borders by the author

Setting by *Infotype (Oxford, England)*

Printing by *Thomson-Shore, Inc. (Dexter, Michigan)*

Manufactured in the United States of America

Distributed by:
Inland Book Company
22 Hemingway Avenue
East Haven, Connecticut 06512

I would like to thank those who gave
me their names as well as their recipes;
and I would also like to thank those who
gave me their recipes without their
names. And a very special thank-you to
John Wayne Keasler of Ball Ground, Georgia;
and Edward Swift of Dime Box, Texas.
E.M.M.

This book is dedicated to
BETTY MAE SWILLEY,
the best cook in Rollin' Fork, Mississippi,
and to ROBERT, who found her
on a tombstone.

CONTENTS

VEGETABLES 'n MEATS (continued)

INTRODUCTION

Never in my whole put-together life could I write down on paper a hard, fast definition of White Trash. Because, for us, as for our southern White Trash cooking, there are no hard and fast rules. We don't like to be hemmed in! But the first thing you've got to understand is that there's white trash and there's White Trash. Manners and pride separate the two. Common white trash has very little in the way of pride, and no manners to speak of, and hardly any respect for anybody or anything. But where I come from in North Florida you never failed to say "yes ma'm" and "no sir," never sat on a made-up bed (or put your hat on it), never opened someone else's icebox, never left food on your plate, never left the table without permission, and never forgot to say "thank you" for the teeniest favor. That's the way the ones before us were raised and that's the way they raised us in the South.

You all know, and we won't let anyone forget it, that the South is legend on top of legend on top of legend. Just read the stories of Eudora Welty, Carson McCullers, William Faulkner, Flannery O'Connor, Truman Capote, and Tennessee Williams. Listen to the songs and stories of Jimmy Rodgers, Mother Maybelle Carter, Hank Williams, Loretta Lynn, Elvis Presley, and Dolly Parton. They all tell us, in their own White Trash ways, that our good times are the best, our bad times are the worst, our tragedies the most extraordinary, our characters the strongest and the weakest, and our humblest meals the most delicious. There ain't much in between. And what really makes us different from others is that we are "in love" with our bad times and weakest characters, we laugh at our worst tragedies, and with a gourmet's delight enjoy our simplest meals. We might tell stories that others think are vulgar or sad, but we make them tales to entertain ourselves and anyone else who will listen. And we always cook enough food for unexpected company. Cooking food, laughing and story telling — that's what we're made of and that's what we enjoy the most.

My mumma died pumping gas at her little filling station/grocery store. Her store was the gathering place. All information, gossip or otherwise, started and stopped at Edna Rae's Grocery Store. If something happened worth gossiping about (and everything was), the store would fill up with people before you could say Jack Robinson. They would all come running out of the palmetto woods, hightailing it for Edna Rae's. She didn't gossip much. She listened and sold groceries and cases of beer and tank upon tank of gas. But in times of misfortune she was always the first to respond. Edna Rae would drag out her cigar box and put a sign on it to collect money for people in need. One sign I clearly remember said, "Please help Iva George and Bertha Sue rebuild their little trailer house. It all burnt down this morning." Then she'd go to the kitchen, and with me to help her she'd cook up a big dinner of fried chittlins, a mess of turnip greens, enough hoe cakes for a Bible story, a wash pot full of swamp cabbage stew, and two large Our Lord's Scripture cakes. Everyone ate in the shade of the shed that covered the gas pumps. When the cigar box was filled to running over with money and all the food was gone, you'd find Iva George and Bertha Sue lazing on the steps of the store, drunk as coots and full as ticks, with lots of company. Bertha Sue's brother, Johnnyboy, saw the trailer burn to the ground. He never talked much until after the fire, but all through dinner he ran around saying, "CRACK and it all burnt down." Mumma said, "He was never really all there." He had some kind of disease when he was a child, and they said, "It eat up part of his brain."

Then there's Big Reba Culpepper, big because there's Little Reba also; Big Reba lives in Burnt Corn, Alabama. She is famous countywide for Reba's Rainbow Icebox Cake. Not too far from Burnt Corn is a place called Flea Hop, Alabama. Big Reba said she has a relative buried "in a small family-type cemetery right out on the edge of town. He was some kind of Civil War hero and when he died he was a very rich man." His grave was richly and clearly marked with a big bronze obelisk "that went way up high," Reba said, "and all his wives (six of them), children, and grandchildren were buried within spittin' distance of his monument. The old cemetery was all growed up with pine trees and needed a whole lot of attention to make it look halfway decent," Reba said. She was afraid if it wasn't cared for someone would steal the big bronze marker. "So I took it on myself to get up a cemetery cleaning party, with rakes, shovels and hoes, fried chicken, Hoppin' John, biscuits, ice tea and, of course, my famous Rainbow Icebox Cake, enough to kill us all. We loaded down the car and took off like Moody's goose for Flea Hop, Alabama." When they reached the cemetery, the marker was gone. She said, ''I wasn't at all surprised. That is, until I found it cemented to the ground in front of the Baptist Church. A cousin said he had moved the marker to the church because they needed something pretty out front and great grandpa's marker was the prettiest thing in Flea Hop. ''Before, the only thing they had in front of the church was an old sign made out of Cocola caps that said, 'Welcome to the Flea Hop Baptist Church.' I couldn't believe they didn't take the body with the marker,'' she said. ''He was embalmed in some kind of special way that was guaranteed for five hundred years. Now they won't even be able to find him.'' Then Reba let out a high-pitched laugh, slapped her leg, and licked the last bit of Rainbow Icebox Cake from her lips.

So you see, telling stories, laughing, and enjoying good food are all deeply rooted in our southern White Trash background. We'll tell any story to make it funny. And we'll bend over backwards to make a good meal: from cooking cooter (turtle) in its shell, to making Vickie's Stickies, to putting up Blackberry Acid in jars (hoping it'll ferment). But rather than runnin' around willy-nilly telling stories (which I could do all day long), it might be quicker to get to what I mean by White Trash cooking if, as Betty Sue says, we go straight to the kitchen and ''get it did.''

If you live in the South or have visited there lately, you know that the old White Trash tradition of cooking is still very much alive, especially in the country. This tradition of cooking is different from ''Soul Food''. White Trash food is not as highly seasoned, except in the coastal areas of South Carolina, Georgia, and North Florida, and along the Gulf coasts of Alabama, Mississippi, Louisiana, and Texas. It's also not as greasy and you don't cook it as long. Of course, there's no denying that Soul Food is a kissin' cousin. All the ingredients are just about the same. But White Trash food, as you'll see by and by, has a great deal more variety.

If someone asked me what sets White Trash cooking aside from other kinds of cooking, I would have to name three of the ingredients: saltmeat, cornmeal, and molasses. Every vegetable eaten is seasoned with saltmeat, bacon, or ham. Cornbread, made with pure cornmeal, is a must with every meal, especially if there's pot liquor. It's also good between meals with a tall glass of cold buttermilk. And many foods are rolled in cornmeal before they are fried. Of course nothing makes cornbread better than a spoon or two of bacon drippings and molasses. For the sweetest pies and pones you ever sunk a tooth into, molasses is the one ingredient you can't find a substitute for. And a little bit of it, used on the side, can top off the flavors of most White Trash food, even a day-old biscuit.

After ingredients, equipment is the next most important thing. As I've said before, there are no hard and fast rules. But skillets, dutch ovens, and cornbread pans (all of black cast iron) are the only utensils that give you that real White Trash flavor and golden brown crust — and that's what you're after. And don't be too concerned about keeping them clean. Netty Irene says, "It's no trouble at all! All you gotta do is rench 'em out, wipe 'em out with a dishrag, and put 'em on the fire to dry out all the water. Then tear off a piece of grocery bag and fold it about two inches square. Dab it in grease and smear it round 'n round the bottom and sides 'til they're plenty covered. Let 'em cool and hang 'em on a nail.'' Netty Irene also said that her mother would never use water on her black iron pots and pans, only dry cornmeal. She'd rub them until they were smooth. She said, "Mamma never threw away the used cornmeal, so she always had another cake of cornbread seasoned and in the makin'.'' Keep your black iron skillet in a good clean condition; it is as special to these recipes as is the wok to Chinese cooking.

Another real common feature of White Trash cooking that sticks out in my mind is that the recipes, because of their deliciousness are swapped and passed around like a good piece of juicy gossip, and by the time they make it back to their source they might be, and almost always are, completely different. Raenelle, Betty Sue's sister-in-law, says, "If I fry down three onions, she's gonna fry down four. If I put in one pack of Jello, she's gonna tump in two." So with every cook trying to outdo the other one, and with all the different tastes, these recipes change so fast it's hard at times to catch them still long enough to get them down on paper. I relied on old family cookbooks, yellowed letters, whispered secrets, and a lot of good hints straight from the kitchens of longtime southern cooks. But I have not written down the endless variations and elaborations on a single dish. And I have not revised the collected recipes unless I had to clarify a very confused situation — and there were a few.

I know you'll lay down and scream when you taste Loretta's Chicken Delight. And Tutti's Fruited Porkettes are fit for the table of a queen. Just how can you miss with a dessert that calls for twenty-three Ritz crackers? And then, there are recipes for coon, possum, and alligator.

These ingredients can even be found in New York City, if you've got an hour and a good taxi driver. You'll be the talk of your social club or sewing circle when you prepare a Resurrection Cake that's guaranteed to resurrect when you pour on the whiskey sauce, or a Grand Canyon Cake or Water Lily Pie that, all going well, look just like their namesakes.

It's not hard to catch on to our ways. Even an awful cook will soon sop them up and become deathly accurate with the sweet potato pones and Miss Bill's Bucket Dumplins. How? No hard, fast rules. Soon you'll find out like the best of the White Trash cooks that there are many ways to fix the same thing, and before long you'll be preparing these dishes with your eyes closed, with the very basics of southern cooking just at your fingertips. I know you'll want to place this cookbook next to the Holy Bible on your coffee table (I know you've got a coffee table with Polaroid snapshots under the glass). And in the kitchen you'll become another Mrs. Betty Sue Swilley, in the true spirit of WHITE TRASH COOKING.

ERNEST MATTHEW MICKLER

ON SERVINGS PER RECIPE

A dear friend of mine, Netta Porter Easterdale, claims to be an expert on portions. She said "All I gotta do is quote my mama." "You take what you've got in the pot and divide it by the number of people you've got to feed or if you only have enough for four everytime another person walks in the door you just add whatever you got the most of to the pot. And it was usually water."

Netta agreed that most of these recipes are for four. "Unless someone tells you different," she said.

Vegetables 'n Meats

UNCLE WILLIE'S SWAMP CABBAGE STEW

1 medium swamp cabbage	2 large chopped onions
3 pieces of fatback	1 teaspoon of white sugar
2 cans of tomatoes	1 pod of hot green pepper,
pinch of thyme	chopped up

Fry fatback, onions, and chopped swamp cabbage til starting to brown. Add tomatoes, sugar, pepper, and thyme. Simmer til it thickens and tomatoes cook down. Add another pinch of thyme 10 minutes before it's done. Serve on rice.

If you don't live along the Carolina, Georgia, North Florida coast, Hearts of Palm in a can will work. But don't cook them too long.

STEWED CABBAGE

1 head of cabbage	3 – 4 slices of fatback or a cup of Virginia smoked ham chunks

Cut up cabbage into quarters, then break the quarters up with your hands. Fry down the meat in a cast-iron dutch oven. Now put cabbage in the pot and fry it down about 10 minutes (turning often). Salt and pepper to taste and add 1 cup of water. Bring it to a boil and then put on the lid and cook 20 minutes on medium low heat or 35 minutes if you like it gray.

Aunt Bertie Mack says you can't cook a good stewed cabbage unless you know how to sing:

Boil that cabbage down boy, boil that cabbage down
Bat your eyes til the crick done rise,
But boil that cabbage down!

BUTTER BEANS (FRESH)

1 quart of fresh butter
   beans
	¼ lb. of bacon, salt meat,
	   or ham

Fry your meat in a pot until it's brown. Pour in the butter beans and add enough water to come up to the top of the beans but not over. Salt and pepper and cook until the beans are tender and the liquid is reduced to half. Serve on rice with pepper vinegar.

    3 lbs. of beans in the shells will give about 1 quart shelled and serves 6. The following list of peas can be cooked just like these beans:
       Crowders
       Purple-hulls
       Field Peas
       Lady Cream Peas (good luck trying to find them)

CREAMED ENGLISH PEAS

Add to canned sweet peas the Yankee Tomato Cream Gravy on page 48. Heat together for 10 minutes and serve with fried chicken or chicken-fried steak.

HOPPIN' JOHN

1 cup raw cowpeas	4 slices bacon fried with
4 cups water	1 medium onion,
2 teaspoons salt	chopped
1 cup raw rice	

Boil peas in salted water until tender. Add peas and 1 cup of the pea liquid to rice, bacon (with grease) and onion. Put in rice steamer or double-boiler and cook for 1 hour or until rice is thoroughly done.

    Black-eyed peas or canned peas will work also if they're already cooked.

LIMPIN' SUSAN

3 – 4 slices of bacon, chopped
  1 pint okra
  1 cup water

1 cup washed rice
salt and pepper to taste

Fry bacon with okra cut in rings. When okra is tender add rice and water, salt and pepper. Put in rice steamer and cook until dry . . . about 1½ hours.
    It just cooks down to nothing.

MATTY MEADE'S CORN AND TOMATOES

1 part whole canned
    tomatoes
1 part whole canned
    kernel corn

½ small onion chopped
    fine
bacon crumbs

Tump together. Simmer til onion is done. Put in a bowl and serve.
    "If you don't like canned vegetables but it's all you got, put a spoon of vinegar in them while they're cookin. Add salt and pepper and a spoon of bacon grease. It'll make 'em almost good as home-canned." *Mrs. Lulamae Bennett, Starke, Florida.*

INDIAN SUCCOTASH

1 pound can green lima
    beans or two cups
    drained
1 tablespoon oleo

1 12 oz. can whole-kernel
    corn, or 1½ cups
    drained
½ cup light cream

Combine, season, and heat.
    Eat with soda crackers spread with mayonnaise.

SUCCOTASH

1 cup fresh corn (cooked)
1 cup fresh lima or butterbeans
1 cup fresh cooked tomatoes

⅓ cup of salt meat or bacon chopped
⅓ cup onions (chopped)

Fry meat. Mix everything together. Add enough water to cover the bottom of the pot. Bring to a boil and serve. Canned is passable, if you've never had the real thing.

CORN ON THE COB

Don't shuck your corn until *just* before you get ready to cook it. Take off the husks, the hairs, and cut off the ends. Rinse it off in fresh water and drop into a big pot of fast boiling water (unsalted). Make sure the water covers all the ears. Wait til your water starts to boil again, then turn off immediately and put on the lid so the flavor won't excape. Now let it sit in the hot water for 5 – 10 minutes (5 for young corn). Drain it and salt it, butter it and eat it.

Mrs. Johnny Keasler of Ball Ground, Georgia, says: "It's the only way to cook your corn on the cob."

CORN OFF THE COB

2 cups of fresh corn or canned

2 tablespoons of butter or bacon grease
salt and pepper

In a skillet, heat the oil and put the corn in to fry. Stir it until it has browned a little. Salt, pepper and serve.

You can add cream (canned or fresh) and corn starch or flour to thicken this if you want to.

You can also add a cup of stewed tomatoes instead of the cream and cook it down.

BAKED SWEET POTATO

Select plump, smooth potatoes. Wash 'em and grease 'em. Put in the oven at 350 degrees for 45 minutes or an hour. They should be soft, through and through, when poked with a fork. Serve hot with butter, make pies or pones or just eat them cold. You can't go wrong.

BOILED PEANUTS

If they're green: put them in a pot, add water to cover and much too much salt. Boil 2 or 3 hours until the hardest ones are tender. Eat 'em as a snack. If they're dried: put them in a pot of water and bring them to a boil. Cut off the fire and let them stand overnight or at least 6 – 8 hours. Then boil in salted water for 4 to 5 hours, until the nut inside the shell is tender. Sometimes you can find them put up in cans in the grocery store.

CHARLYSS'S BLACK-EYED PEAS
(OR, WHOLE-GRAINED CORN)

Get yourself a good, non-stick cooking pot and put it over a medium flame. Put in 5 or 6 good heaping tablespoons full of olive oil and allow to heat for a few minutes (2 or 3). Chop up 2 (or 3) good-sized onions and put into the pot. Stir slowly and thoroughly, being careful to mix in a healthy one-half handful of chopped parsley a few minutes after you've added the onions to the pot. Continue to sauté these ingredients for 2 to 3 minutes; then cover and lower flame to slightly under medium. Every 4 to 5 minutes lift the pot cover and stir slowly. While the onions and parsley are cooking slowly, chop about 3 cups full of ham (or thick bacon bits) and add to pot, carefully stirring everything together thoroughly. Open 3 large cans of black-eyed peas. After the onions, parsley and ham pieces have been cooking for about 10 – 15 minutes, add all

3 cans of peas to the pot, stir thoroughly, cover, and cook over a medium flame for about 30 to 45 minutes until tender. Then serve over freshly cooked rice. Serves 3 or 4 hungry people.

Charlyss, the cook and owner of the Side Board Restaurant in Cut-off, Louisiana, feeds a lot of very hungry men. And they keep coming back. "They say it's the only place where you can get filled up and satisfied too."

BONNIE'S BLACK-EYED PEAS

1¼ cups of dried black-eyed
     peas
4 cups of water

1 cup chopped salt pork
    or fatback
1 medium onion (chopped)

Put together in pot and cook 3 hours or more (boil slowly). When they are soft, remove one cup and mash well and return them to the pot and salt and pepper to taste. Serve over boiled rice with greens and a meat. Some people enjoy cut-up raw onions and pepper vinegar sprinkled over the top of the peas.

With the leftovers you can make a real quick Hoppin' John by mixing the leftover peas and meat with the leftover rice. Heat and serve for another meal. In Louisiana they call this a Jambalaya.

RED BEANS & RICE

2 lbs. dried red beans
   (kidney)
2 cups chopped yellow
   onions
1 bunch of scallions (green
   onions), chopped
3 – 4 finely sliced cloves of
   garlic

1 bunch parsley (chopped)
3 lbs. of a good smoked
   sausage cut into 2 inch
   lengths (smoked ham or
   ham bone works fine)
salt and pepper to taste
3 quarts of cold water

Soak beans overnight if possible. Drain water and add beans to a large 8 – 10 quart pot. Then add enough of the cold water to cover the beans. Add chopped yellow onions and garlic and bring to a boil. Cook one hour and add all the other things and more water if necessary. Simmer (slight bubbling action) for 2 more hours or until beans are soft. Then remove 2 cups of cooked beans without juice and mash very good. Then return the mashed up beans to the pot and stir into the mixture. This makes a creamy, thicker gravy. If the beans are too dry, add enough water to make them like you like them. Good over boiled rice. Serves 8.

If you're in New Orleans on Monday, this is the only thing you can eat.

SNAP BEANS

String and snap 2 lbs. of green beans into 1½ inch pieces. Put in a pot with fatback (bacon) or ham hocks. Add a double handful of little new potatoes or 3 to 4 medium ones cut into quarters. Now cover with water, add salt and pepper to taste and cook on a medium-slow fire until the beans are tender and the liquid has cooked down to half.

THE DUTCHESS'S BAKED BEANS

(by Gloria de Long)

3 cups home-cooked beans of any kind (3 cups of Campbell's pork 'n beans will do in a pinch)
1 cup chopped onions

½ teaspoon cinnamon
1 cup ketchup
enough bacon slices to cover the top

Put your beans in a bowl. Mix everything together except bacon slices. Salt and pepper to taste, pour out into a flat baking dish or pan. Cover top with bacon slices and stick it in a 350-degree oven for 35 minutes, or until some of the juice is gone. That's it.

For cooking white beans (Navy, Greater Northern, Lima and others)

1 1 lb. sack of beans
1 big ham hock (or picnic ham bone with a little meat left on it)
1 big yellow onion chopped

2 quarts of water
   salt and pepper (as much as you want)

Some people add a spoon of sugar, soda, or nutmeg.

Put your beans, water and ham hock in a pot. Bring your water to a rolling boil. Turn the fire down to low. Let 'em cook for two and a half hours or until when you mash 'em up they're tender.

If you need to add water, always make sure it's hot. All Cajuns add a handful of chopped green onions and chopped parsley 20 minutes before beans are done. (For shorter cooking time, soak them overnight.)

BETTY SUE'S FRIED OKRA

1 lb. of fresh okra or 2 packages of frozen (cut in rounds)

1 ½ cups corn meal or cracker meal
     salt, pepper (heavy salt)

Salt and pepper okra, then shake it in a brown paper sack with 1 ½ cups of meal til okra is all covered. Heat skillet very hot with ⅓ cup of oil. Put in okra and fry to golden brown (12 minutes or thereabout). Remove from skillet and lay okra on paper towel to absorb excess oil. Serve hot. Enough for 4.

"Steer clear of all those fancy frozen packages of this-in-a-sack or that-in-a-sack. Loose frozen vegetables are just as good, but make sure you season them like you like them," says Mrs. Swilley.

BETTY SUE'S SISTER-IN-LAW'S FRIED EGGPLANT

Wash eggplant in cold water and then peel. Cut it up into round slices ½ inch thick. Dip it in a mixture of 1 egg and ½ cup of milk, and then dredge it in salted-and-peppered cracker meal. Fry in a heavy frying pan in a light oil until golden on both sides. 3 – 4 persons per large eggplant.

If you don't have cracker meal, use corn meal. If you don't have corn meal, use flour.

FRIED CUCUMBER

2 large cucumbers (cut length-wise)	salt
1 ½ cups of corn meal	pepper

Salt and pepper the cucumbers. Shake in a brown paper sack with 1 ½ cups of corn meal until the cucumbers are covered. Heat ⅓ cup of oil in a very hot skillet. Add cucumbers and fry until golden brown. Remove cucumbers and put on a paper towel to absorb excess oil.

Serves 4 or 5.

FRIED SQUASH

3 large zucchini (cut into rounds)	1 ½ cups of corn meal

Cook the same as fried okra and cucumbers.

HOME FRIES

1 medium-to-large potato for each person you're serving. Peel and slice them into rounds ⅛ inch thick.

In an iron frying pan heat ¼ or ½ inch of grease until it begins to bubble. Now add your potatoes until they cover the bottom of the pan. Fry on both sides until medium golden-brown. Drain them on paper towels. Salt and serve.

For *French Fries*, cut into sticks and fry as you do Home Fries.

MINDA LYNN'S COLD POTATO SALAD

5 – 7 potatoes cubed and boiled

½ cup mayo (sometimes more is best)

¼ cup onion all chopped up

1 teaspoon mustard (sometimes more, sometimes less)

2 – 3 great big sour pickles all chopped up

several hard-boiled eggs all chopped up (5 will do, but 8 make a richer salad)

pickle juice to taste

salt to taste

pepper to taste

Put all ingredients together in a big pan and mix it up. If you need more moisture, add more pickle juice, or a little bit of milk, or mayonnaise. If you need more onion, chop it up and put it in. If you need more pickles, put them in too, but remember they're hard to take out. Some people like more mustard than mayonnaise and a whole lot of eggs. Then it's real, real yellow. Some people like more mayonnaise than mustard and then it's not quite so tart.

Minda Lynn swears you can do anything you want to with this salad, depending on your mood. But she advises to always take the skins off your potatoes because, if you leave them on, the salad will look awfully dirty.

SPUDS HOT POTATO SALAD

4 – 5 large potatoes
½ cup of can cream
2 large spoons of Blue
   Plate mayonnaise
3 large eggs, hard-boiled
2 heaping teaspoons of
   French's mustard

1 medium onion cut up
   in thin pieces
salt and black pepper
   to taste

Peel potatoes and cube in large pieces. Put in pot and boil until they're soft through and through. (You can boil your eggs with the potatoes if you want to.) When potatoes are soft, drain the water and then mash like mashed potatoes. Set aside. Cut up onion and cut up eggs. Add them to the potatoes along with cream, mayonnaise, mustard, salt, and black pepper. Mix thoroughly and serve hot.

This recipe is from Spuds, Florida. According to Mrs. Myrtle Batten it's the potato capital of the world.

SCALLOPED POTATOES & ONIONS

4 – 5 large potatoes
2 large onions
4 tablespoons of oleo

2 cups of milk
salt and pepper

Into a baking dish put a layer of thin sliced potatoes, salt, pepper, and dots of oleo. Then add a layer of thin sliced onions. Cover these with more dots of oleo, salt and pepper. Repeat until all potatoes and onions are used. Pour enough milk over potatoes and onions to cover them. Cook in a moderate oven until potatoes are well browned on the top. These proportions may be varied according to the size of the dish and the number of people you gotta feed.

MAMMY'S MASHED POTATOES

Peel 4 or 5 medium-to-large potatoes and dice into ½ to 1 inch cubes. Boil in just enough water to cover them up and throw in a teaspoon of salt to bring out the flavor. When forked and they're tender all the way through (30 minutes usually), drain off the water, then mash them up with your masher until there are no more lumps. Add a tablespoon of butter and two tablespoons of cream (canned or other). Serve hot with brown gravy.

MAMMY'S COLORED MASHED POTATOES

Boil ½ lb. carrots (3 or 4) and ½ lb. potatoes. Mash potatoes and carrots together and follow Mammy's Mashed Potato recipe. They look so pretty and bright the children will love them and grown-ups too.

There are many potato mashers on the market but, according to Mammy, the best one there is is a quart fruit jar. "The bottom's not too large and not too small. Mashes 'em up real good."

EDNA RAE'S SMOTHERED POTATOES

4 medium potatoes, sliced   red pepper
    in rounds ¼ inch thick   salt
1 onion, or 1 bunch of
    scallions, chopped

Fry onions in cast-iron skillet in 2 tablespoons of bacon grease or other cooking oils until limp and kind of brown. Add potatoes and stir til all of them are covered in oil and starting to brown. Add 1 cup of water, salt, and pepper. Put lid on and cook til potatoes are soft and brown in some places. Then add green onions and red pepper and cook 10 minutes more. Serve with pork or fried chicken.

"Let them get a real brown crust on bottom without burnin', that's the trick," Edna Rae says.

NETTY IRENE'S MACARONI & CHEESE

4 cups cooked elbow
   macaroni
1 cup grated or chunked
   yellow cheese
3 eggs
1 cup Carnation evaporated
   milk (no substitute,
   please)

10 bacon strips (or enough
   to cover)
salt and pepper

Blend the eggs and milk together and pour into macaroni already in a flat pyrex baking dish. Put in the cheese and poke it around until thoroughly mixed. Salt it to taste. Then put enough black pepper to coat it all real good. Place on bacon slices and cook in 350-degree oven until it gets a good crust on top and has hardened a little. About 30 – 40 minutes. Don't cook it too long, you want it runny in between the elbows.

"This recipe is from Miss Myrtle Talmadge's Home-Ec class and I made it for the Senior Prom Dinner. It was so good I been makin' it ever since," Netty told me.

ONION PIE

½ stick oleo, melted

2 large onions, chopped up

Fry onions in oleo until limp, but don't brown. Let 'em cool slightly and add 1 tablespoon flour, ⅓ can evaporated milk, ⅛ teaspoon salt and one cup of sweet milk. Cook all above ingredients until thick. Beat three eggs in a bowl and add to mixture. Pour into 9-inch unbaked pie-shell. Top with another pie-shell. Brush with milk. Bake at 425 degrees for 30 – 40 minutes.

Serve with Ham-Lima Salad found on page 65.

MIKE MITCHELL'S GRANDMOTHER'S SPINACH PIE

1 lb. or bunch of fresh
  spinach or
1 lb. can of spinach,
  drained
2 eggs
2 tablespoons of chopped
  onion/green scallions
2 tablespoons of evaporated
  milk

4 oz. sharp cheddar cheese
salt and pepper
2 pie crusts (one for pan
  and other for top)
2 tablespoons of butter

Fresh spinach: Fry spinach and onion in the butter til onions are transparent and spinach wilted.
Canned spinach: Fry onions and add spinach.

Beat eggs and milk with a fork and add to spinach and onions. Put in an uncooked pie-shell and cover the spinach mixture with the slices of cheese ¼ inch thick. Then put the other pie crust on top and bake for 15 or 25 minutes (or until top is brown) at 350 degrees.

Serve hot. Enough for 6.

MARY BETH BONEY'S COLLARD GREENS

Wash your collards 3 or 4 times in fresh water, draining them each time. (There's nothing worse than gritty collards.) Then strip the leafy part from the stems and throw the stems to the chickens, if you got any. In a large pot fry down 1 lb. of fatback, thick bacon, or ham chunks til brown. Then add collards. Stir and fry all this until collards start to wilt. Add 2 cups of water and cook until tender. Add more water if necessary. Some people like a spoon of sugar in the water to sweeten the greens. Stir frequently on medium heat so they don't burn.

OLETA BROWN'S TURNIP GREENS

Manage the same as collards, but you can add the turnip bottoms to the greens for cooking. Just peel them and cut them into 2-inch chunks. Delicious with black-eyed peas, ham hocks, and corn bread.

MUSTARD GREENS

Manage the same as collards but cooking time is shorter (usually).

Coleta Davis always cooks her mustard, collards and turnips together in one big pot and seasoned with bacon fat.

TANYA (ELEPHANT EARS)

Pare the tanya root as you would a turnip. Cook in saucepan with cold water and bring to a boil. Pour the water off, add more cold water and a little salt, and cook until tender. Slice and serve hot with drawn butter.

CRÊPES À LA CREOLA LE BEAU

1 can Campbell's Cream
  of Mushroom Soup
½ cup mayonnaise
  collard greens (left-over
  collards are best)

crêpes (go buy a package
  of flour tortillas)

Cook soup (DO NOT THIN) and mayonnaise til hot. Fill crêpes with left-over collards. Pour the sauce over them and serve.

COLD COLLARD SANDWICH

Use enough ice-cold, left-over collard greens to cover a slice of light bread. Sprinkle on some pepper vinegar to taste. Then cover the other slice of bread generously with Blue Plate mayonnaise and eat.

This is truly a southern delicacy since there are seldom any collards left.

MARY LINDER'S WASHDAY SOUP

Put Navy beans in a big pot of salted water to soak overnight. Put on with the wash water about six in the morning, with bacon, or ham. Let cook uncovered on low burner. Clock between loads of wash. Add 1 large, finely minced onion at eight when you're blueing the overalls. At nine have a quick cup of coffee and dump ½ cup in the beans if you want. Add ½ cup fine minced carrots at bleach time (about eleven). Serve at noon with soda crackers and slaw you made the night before. For washday this is a pretty good deal.

HOMEMADE VEGETABLE SOUP

1 cup corn
1 cup green beans
1 can stewed tomatoes
2 cups of potatoes (cut up)
2 cups of yellow onions
  (cut up)

1 beef soup bone
1 cup of stew meat (beef)
2 toes of garlic
  salt and black pepper or
    tabasco to taste

Put everything in a soup pot and cover with water (about 2 inches over the vegetables). Cook until meat and vegetables are falling apart. Add 1 bunch of green onions (chopped), ½ bunch of parsley (chopped). Cook 20 minutes more and taste of it to see if it's ready to serve. Soda crackers or cornbread?

MOCK COOTER SOUP

3 pounds lean beef or
   ground meat
1 pint sweet milk
1 tablespoon flour
½ teaspoon mace
   salt and pepper to taste

½ teaspoon dry mustard
1½ quarts of water
¼ pound of oleo
½ pint cream
2 hard-boiled eggs cut up
   in medium-size chunks

Boil meat and water until one quart of liquid remains. Add one pint of milk and ¼ pound oleo. Remove meat, allow to cool, grind and return to stock. Let it cook down a little more. Add flour dissolved in cream. Add seasonings. Refer to Cooter section for the real thing.

   Mrs. Ina Filker of Sandfly, Georgia, says "Give you a silver dollar if you kin tell the difference."

PORE FOLK SOUP

For a light supper, crumble soda crackers in warm milk. Salt, pepper, and eat with a spoon.

Hooka tooka my soda crackers?
Does yer Mammy chaw tobaccer?
If yer Mammy chaw tobaccer then
Then Hooka tooka my soda cracker?

BRENDA'S BLACK BEAN SOUP

2 cups black beans
1 ham bone
2 ribs celery
½ teaspoon pepper
4 tablespoons oleo
3 tablespoons sherry
2 quarts water

2 tablespoons chopped
   onion
2 teaspoons salt
¼ teaspoon dry mustard
1½ tablespoons flour
1 lemon, thin-sliced

Soak beans overnight. Drain, add to water and ham bone. Cook onion in one-half the oleo (2 tablespoons). Add onion and celery to beans and simmer three to four hours in covered kettle (until beans are soft). Re-heat to boiling, add salt, pepper, mustard and remaining oleo, and flour.

MRS. HENRY DORSEY SHORT'S REAL COUNTRY-SMOKED HAM

1. Soak in water overnight (covered).
2. Scrub.
3. Put in roaster with:
   6 cups water
   1 cup bourbon
   1 handful sugar.
Simmer until you can wiggle the bone.

PORK ROAST

Take a sharp knife and stick holes in the roast and stuff each hole with a sliver of garlic. The holes should be about 1½ – 2 inches apart. Then rub the roast with lots of salt, pepper and a little brown sugar. Have your dutch oven on the stove with just enough grease to brown the roast on all sides. Surround it with sweet potatoes (whole). Cover it and cook slowly until the pork is tender and *well done*. If you need some juice, use a little water.

Some people brown their pork roast on top of the stove and then put it in the oven. It takes a little longer but they say it's better.

PORK CHOPS

Cut the excess fat off the chops. Salt and pepper them. Douse them in flour and fry in hot grease over medium heat until they're golden brown and *well done*, but not dry.

Make gravy from the drippins (page 47).

Make sure you look after the pork chops with some good Motts apple sauce or pickled apples.

TUTTI'S FRUITED PORKETTES

1 pound sweet potatoes	6 tender pork chops
12 slices canned pineapple	6 tablespoons brown
6 slices bacon, cut into	sugar
halves	

Select sweet potatoes to make slices a bit smaller than pineapple slices. Cut into slices 1 inch thick. Parboil the potatoes in salted water for 10 minutes. Place each chop between two slices of pineapple. Place slice of sweet potato on top of each pork-pineapple stack. Sprinkle each porkette with one tablespoon of brown sugar. Place bacon crisscross on top. Place porkettes in open casserole. Bake at 375 degrees for one hour or longer, depending on thickness of chops.

Tutti, Petie's grandma, said ''she learned to make her porkettes by using a Hawaiian recipe combined with Southern ingredients. You cain't git trashier than that.''

SAUERKRAUT & SPARERIBS

1 large can sauerkraut (drained)	2 lbs. spareribs

Get the butcher to chop the spareribs into 2 – 3 inch links. Salt and pepper them. Then in a heavy bottom pot, heat ⅛ inch grease and brown the spareribs on all sides. Add sauerkraut, cover and cook until the ribs are tender and coming off the bone. Serve with Mammy's Mashed Potatoes.

SINGLE BOY'S BREAKFAST

Take one pound of pork sausages. Cook them evenly, pour off fat. Add one and one half box soda crackers (unsalted) crumbled. Pour in one cup of boiling water. Cover tight and steam five minutes. Serve with fried sweet potatoes and plenty of hot, black coffee.

FRESH FRIED SWEET POTATOES

Peel and slice the sweet potatoes lengthwise and place immediately in a heated iron frying pan with ¼ inch of grease. Fry until golden brown and soft in the middle when poked by a fork. Goes good with sausage or bacon.

NOBODY'S CORN TOPPER CASSEROLE

(made with ham)

1 1 pound can cut green beans, drained	4 tablespoons finely-chopped onion
1 can cream of mushroom soup	2 cups cubed cooked ham
1 1 pound can cream-style corn	¾ cup prepared biscuit mix (Bisquick)

Place beans in a 2-quart greased casserole, reserving a few for garnish. Sprinkle onion on top; spread with soup. Top with a layer of ham. Bake at 425 degrees for 15 to 20 minutes. Combine corn and biscuit mix. Spoon mixture on top of casserole. Bake for 15 – 20 minutes longer. Garnish with rest of beans.

CHICKEN-FRIED STEAK

round steak	pepper
flour	Crisco, or vegetable oil
salt	of your choice

Take a piece of round steak about as big as a slice of bread and twice as thick. Beat it with the back of a knife* until it's thin, scarred and tender. Then sprinkle it with salt, pepper and flour it on both sides. Flour it until it's all white and you can't see a trace of meat anywhere. (You just about can't get too much.) Now you're ready to fry it on both sides in about ½ inch of hot grease.

Chicken-fried steak should always be cooked *well* done.

Serve with white gravy (below) and mashed potatoes, a slab of lettuce, a wedge of tomato, and crisscross the french fries.

*Pearl Brown always used the edge of a real thick saucer to tenderize her steak. "Be careful not to break it," she always said.

WHITE GRAVY (WITH MILK)

To make a good white milk gravy you've gotta have a good eye for measurements. After you fry your chicken or steak, look at the drippins in the pan and try to decide just how much flour and milk you need to thicken it up without getting too much. If you have just fried a good-sized chicken, or several pieces of steak, and you've got a fair amount of drippins in the skillet, then you'll probably use 2 tablespoons of flour with about ¼ cup of milk. Mix it until there're no more lumps and then add it to the drippins and stir over a low flame until thick. If you get your gravy too thick, just water it down some; if it's too thin, add some more flour. Always keep reminding yourself that it takes years of practice to make a good flour gravy. Nobody's perfect right at the very first.

POT ROAST

Heavily salt and pepper the roast on both sides, then flour it. Put it into a hot dutch oven with about ⅛ inch lard. Sear and fry until golden brown on all sides. This seals in the flavor. Cover with carrots, potatoes, and onions (whole or cut up). Put on the lid and cook on a slow fire until meat and vegetables are tender. If the meat does not have enough juice of its own, add a little bit of water.

Remove the meat and use drippins for gravy (page 47).

SMOTHERED LIVER'N ONIONS

Take 1 pound of calves' liver and cut into 3 or 4-inch squares. Salt, pepper and flour it (coat it real good). Fry it in your skillet in ¼ inch of hot grease until it's done (golden brown). Take out the liver and pour off the grease and make gravy (see page 47).

Put your liver back in the skillet with enough gravy to just barely cover it. Now cover the top with sliced onion rings. Put a lid on it and simmer until the onions are done.

Serve with ketchup.

INLAND BEEF STEW

2 lbs. stew meat (cubed)	2 large onions (chopped)
4 large carrots (hunked)	1 toe garlic (crushed)
4 large potatoes (hunked)	¾ cup flour

In a large enough stew pot or dutch oven, fry down your meat in bacon grease until browned, and then add onion and fry until limp and you can see through them. Add the carrots, potatoes and garlic, cover with water, then salt and pepper to taste. Leave this on the fire and forget about it for a little while.

Now put the flour in an iron skillet and turn the stove on high. Push and stir the flour with a flat-ended spatula until it's deep brown but not burned. Then put it into the stew and stir until all lumps are gone. Cook the stew awhile and if it's too thick add a little water. If it's too thin cook it down until it's thick. When it's ready the meat should be tender and the vegetables falling apart. Serve over rice.

For *Coastal Beef Stew*, add a cup of stewed tomatoes, 3 bay leaves, ½ teaspoon of ground thyme, 2 more toes of garlic and a hot pepper. If you do this, you land up with a livelier stew.

Another variation is to use chicken stock instead of water, if you think the stew meat doesn't have enough flavor. Dana Kay Pullen said she discovered this by accident.

BRUNSWICK STEW

5 pounds beef
5 pounds chicken
2½ pounds pork
5 pounds Irish potatoes
4 pounds of onions
2 quarts of lima beans
4 quarts of tomatoes
2 quarts of Niblet corn
1 quart okra
1 bottle of Worcestershire sauce (10 oz. size)
¼ teaspoon allspice
6 Sunkist lemons (juice only)
1 tablespoon of white sugar
1 pod of hot pepper or 1 teaspoon tabasco sauce (more if you want it real hot)
2 bottles of ketchup
1 tablespoon of French's prepared mustard
¼ teaspoon cloves
¼ cup white vinegar
1 tablespoon of liquid hickory smoke
1½ gallons of chicken-and-meat juice

Cook beef, chicken, and pork in pot covered with water until tender. Let cool. Grind in meat grinder. Grind the potatoes and onions; add to meat and juice. Cook 30 minutes. Add other ingredients as listed. Mix well. Cook 1½ hours, stirring often. If canning, cook only 30 minutes. Place in jars. Process 60 minutes at 15 pounds pressure or 90 minutes at 10 pounds pressure. If freezing, let cool, place in containers and freeze. Or serve hot with rice and corn pone.

Good for a family reunion or church supper.

AUNT ROSIE DEATON'S ALL-AMERICAN SLUM-GULLION (The Best)

Cook some elbow macaroni — plenty. Brown minced onion (stronger the better), hamburger and/or bacon in a skillet. Add 1 can of whole Delmonte tomatoes, salt, pepper and all the macaroni you got. Simmer til you can't stand it any more, then take it off the fire and dive in. This is especially good when you're in a hurry-up day, like when there's a funeral, an auction, or a flag-burning at the Legion Hall.

CHILI

½ sack pinto beans, cooked
   until tender
2 onions chopped
1 bottle ketchup
1 pound hamburger meat

2 cans tomatoes
chili powder to taste,
   cayenne powder to
   taste, salt and pepper
   to taste

Cook pintos until tender. Brown meat and onions. Add to beans. Add tomatoes and ketchup and the other ingredients; cayenne, salt, and pepper to taste. Makes large dutch oven full.

JAIL-HOUSE CHILI

3 pounds diced lean beef
¼ cup Wesson oil
1 quart water
8 chili pods or 6
   tablespoons chili powder
3 teaspoons salt
5 cloves finely chopped
   garlic
1 teaspoon ground cumin

1 teaspoon marjoram
1 teaspoon red pepper
1 tablespoon white sugar
3 tablespoons paprika
To Thicken
3 tablespoons flour
6 tablespoons white corn
   meal
1 cup water

Heat oil in large pot, add meat and sear over high heat. Stir constantly until meat is gray but not brown. Add water and cover, cooking over low fire for 1½ to 2 hours. Add remaining ingredients, except for thickening, and cook at a bubbling simmer for 30 minutes. Add thickening which has previously been mixed with 1 cup of water. Cook about 5 more minutes, hand stir to prevent sticking. More water may be added if it's too thick. If meat is very fat, skim off fat before adding thickening. This is really hot chili.

CORN BEEF & HASH

1 can of corn beef
1 can of tomatoes
3 medium potatoes (cubed)
1 large onion (chopped)

1 teaspoon of sugar
2 slices of fatback
1 bayleaf

Fry down onion and fatback til limp, then add potatoes and fry (stirring often) til brown. Add meat, tomatoes, sugar, and bayleaf. Salt and pepper to taste and serve over grits or rice.

"So good it'll make your tongue slap your jaw teeth out," says Edna Rae Mills.

SLOPPY JOE'S ON CORN BREAD

1 pound ground beef
½ cup chopped bell pepper
1 grated carrot
1 can tomato puree or
   ketchup
1 teaspoon black pepper

¾ cup chopped onions
½ cup chopped celery
1 No. 2 can Libby's
   tomatoes
¾ teaspoon salt

Brown ground beef in big iron skillet. Stir in onion, bell pepper, celery, and fry until brown. Add carrot, tomatoes and puree. Stir mixture well, season with salt and pepper. Simmer for one hour and serve hot over hot-buttered cornbread. Serves 6.

"If you're using day-old cornbread, put it in a pie pan and use it for a lid while the Sloppy Joe's cooks. Everything'll be ready at the same time." — *Mildred Louise McQuaig.*

DIRTY RICE

1 lb. of ground beef	1 cup of rice
1 large onion (chopped)	

Brown the ground meat and onions in bacon fat. Salt and pepper to taste. Add the rice covered with water, boil 1 minute while stirring. Put a lid on it and cook until the rice is fluffy and dry. About 25 – 30 minutes.

For *Spicy Dirty Rice* use 3 cloves of garlic, 2 peppers, ¼ pound chicken livers (chopped), 1 tablespoon Worcestershire sauce, a handful of green onions (chopped), and 2 tablespoons of parsley (chopped).

"After you've handled onions, get rid of that awful smell by rubbing lemon all over your hands." — *Eva Gay Ashworth, Pt. Neches, Texas.*

DANA PULLEN'S CHICKEN FEET & RICE

You can't get chicken feet at the supermarket these days,* so you gotta go to a butcher store and beg for them. (They're usually thrown away.) Once you get them, rinse them off, drop them into a pot of hot boiling water for five minutes and then take them out and the outer skin will just roll right off. Make sure you get it all off because there's no telling where the chicken's been walkin'. Now that the skin is cleaned off, take your cast iron dutch oven, cover the bottom with oil, put in the feet and fry til golden brown. Then put in a handful of chopped onions and one toe of garlic (flattened). Fry the onions until you can see through them, put in the desired amount of rice (depending on the number of people you're feeding), and cover with water. Salt, pepper, and bring to a boil. Put the lid on and cook the rice til fluffy and the chicken feet are tender.

The only way to eat a chicken foot is to gnaw on it. The round ball of the foot is the best part. They are a gristly kind of thing and can be used in soups, but when you fry them they're really good.

Serve with potato salad, greens, and biscuits.

Even though Miss Pullen says you can't find chicken feet in the supermarkets, we have talked to a lot of people who have seen them there.

SOUTHERN FRIED CHICKEN

You take a chicken and ya kill it
And you put it in the skillet
And you fry to a golden brown
That's Southern Cookin'
And it's mighty fine

According to Ernestine Mills, you take a good-sized chicken and cut it up the way you like it. Roll the pieces in salt and black pepper (plenty) and then roll it in flour until heavily coated. Heat grease (¼ cup bacon and ¾ cup vegetable oil) in a black iron skillet until a small bit dropped in jumps back at you.

Then put in enough chicken pieces to cover the skillet, but not too crowded. Fry it to a deep golden brown on one side and then turn it over. Lower heat til it simmers, and then fry that side to a golden brown. Takes about 35 minutes. Turn again if you see blood.

Serve with potato salad, rice, and chicken gravy made from the drippins (page 47).

SMOTHER-FRIED CHICKEN

Cut up one chicken; salt, pepper and flour it. Fry til golden brown in iron frying pan, remove it from the grease and make Mamma's Gravy (page 47). Then put chicken back in the frying pan with the gravy and smother for 20 minutes over medium heat.

If you have any Col. Sanders left over, make a gravy and throw it in. Smother for 20 – 30 minutes.

MARGIE'S FRIED CHICKEN

Cut up fryer, clean with lemon only. Dredge in a mixture of flour, salt, pepper, and allspice. Put in ½ inch of hot lard. Fry one side then the other until well done. Eat directly out of the skillet. This is very good with a cold beer. If you're a strict Baptist, have a lemonade or a cold drink, and may Gold bless your home.

PEARL'S CHICKEN & CORNBREAD DRESSING

Cook two pans of cornbread two days before you're going to fix your chicken and let it get hard in the refrigerator or on top of the stove. On the day your company's coming, you take a good fat hen and boil her down until you've got about three cups of rich chicken stock. Sometimes you need more, sometimes you need less.

Then, in a roasting pan, crumble up your two-day-old cornbread and mix with green onions all cut up, celery all cut up, boiled eggs all cut up, and some green pepper if you like it. All this is done to taste. Then add salt and pepper to taste and then add your boiled chicken, being careful to place her in the center of the pan. When she's positioned on her back you pour in the chicken stock, just enough to wet the cornbread if you like your dressing on the dry side, and if you like it on the wet side then you simply add some more stock. Next pop the bird (uncovered) in the oven (about 350 – 400) and when the dressing is hot through and through, or when it starts to bubble, take it out and start eating.

Serve with canned cranberry sauce, a green vegetable of your choice and sweet potatoes.

EVELYN WALTER'S NEVER-FAIL, SUNDAY BAKED CHICKEN

Take any old chicken. Clean with lemon only. Stuff; place in a baking dish or skillet; cover with a rag soaked in lard or Crisco. Bake at 275 degrees til tender and brown.

Stuffing: 2 cups dry bread, 2 cup chopped celery, 2 eggs, ½ teaspoon salt, ½ tablespoon pepper, 1 small package walnuts, 1 small chopped apple, 1 teaspoon of sage and a pinch of dry mustard. Pour drippins from baked chicken on stuffing mixture. Mix together and stuff. If not moist enough, add water.

"Don't turn the oven any higher or the rag'll catch on fire," says Evelyn, Kansas City, Mo.

CHICKEN STEW (WHITE)

1 chicken (cut for frying)
1 cup of chopped onions
1 cup of chopped celery
   corn starch or flour
    for thickening

salt and pepper to taste
2 tablespoons of bacon
   grease

In a dutch oven, heat the bacon grease and stir in the onions and celery. Fry them until they're limp but not beginning to brown. Add chicken parts and fry until the color has changed to white. Cover about 1 to 2 inches with water and cook until the meat is tender. Thicken if necessary. Serve over rice or make dumplings in the stew.

CHICKEN STEW (BROWN)

1 chicken (cut up)
1 bunch of green onions
   (chopped)
1 bunch of parsley
   (chopped)

¾ cup flour
½ cup bacon grease or oil
   salt, pepper, and tabasco
    to taste

Put drippins in a dutch oven and heat. Add flour and brown it to a rich brown, stirring constantly. Put the onions and parsley in the flour and add a little more oil if it's too stiff to stir. Cook a few minutes and add chicken parts and enough water barely to cover. Put in salt, pepper and tabasco to taste and mix everything real good. Put a lid on it and cook until the meat is just before leaving the bone. Serve over rice with corn and greens.

    This is very good with half-dollar-size dumplings made in the stew. You may need more liquid. If you do, just go ahead and add it.

MEMPHIS WOOD'S COVERED CHICKEN

Take some frying-size pieces of chicken. Salt and pepper them very good. Now smear with mustard until covered. Roll up each piece, individually, in tin foil and seal. Put 'em in a preheated oven at 400 degrees for 35-40 minutes.

Meanwhile, take out your corn for boiling, and your can spinach for heating, and your dinner's ready.

Serve the chicken in tin foil (2 or 3 per person). The kids will love unwrapping their own.

"I'd like to stress the point of being very generous with the French's mustard and when it's done, open it up and brown it under the broiler for an even more delicious flavor. Don't forget some Bisquick biscuits in that same oven, because they're as good as homemade. I use a lots of packaged things all the time, if they're good." — *Memphis.*

LORETTA'S CHICKEN DELIGHT

1 No. 14 can asparagus	2½ cups chopped cooked chicken
1 small can pimiento, chopped	3 hard-cooked eggs, sliced
¼ pound soda crackers, crumbled	1 can cream of chicken soup
½ soup can of water	¾ stick oleo

Place a layer of asparagus in bottom of greased casserole; add a layer of chicken, pimiento, eggs, and cracker crumbs. Repeat. Dilute soup with water; pour over casserole. Sprinkle with additional crumbs. Place slices of oleo over top. Bake at 375 degrees for 30 minutes.

ESTHER'S CHICKEN CASSEROLE MADE FROM SCRATCH

1 stewing hen	6 – 7 cups salted water
3 heaping tablespoons flour	salt and pepper
1 onion, diced	2 cups diced celery
3 tablespoons oleo or	8 slices toast, diced
Wesson oil	½ teaspoon poultry
½ teaspoon Calumet baking	seasoning
powder	2 eggs, slightly beaten
dash of curry powder	dash of yellow food
1½ cups sweet milk	coloring

Cook chicken in water until tender; remove chicken from bone. Reserve 4 cups stock and add food coloring. Thicken reserved stock with flour. Season to taste. Place chicken in casserole; pour thickened stock over chicken. Brown onion and celery in oil, adding remaining ingredients. Season to taste with salt and pepper. Place on top of chicken. Bake at 325 degrees for 45 minutes to 1 hour.

FREDA'S FIVE-CAN CASSEROLE

1 small can boneless	1 small can evaporated
chicken	milk
1 can cream of mushroom	1 small onion, minced
soup	½ cup diced celery
1 can Chinese noodles	½ cup sliced almonds
1 can chicken with rice	
soup	

Mix all ingredients; place in casserole. Bake at 350 degrees for 1 hour.

LADY DIVINE'S CHICKEN-ASPARAGUS PIE

½ package dehydrated
onion soup mix
1 can cream of chicken
soup
1 cooked chicken, boned
and cut into large
pieces
¼ cup shredded Parmesan
cheese

1 cup sour cream
2 pounds fresh-from-the-
garden asparagus, or
1 can cooked and
drained
1 cup heavy cream,
whipped

Add soup mix to sour cream; beat with rotary beater until well blended. Beat in soup. Arrange cooked asparagus spears cross-wise in a large, deep, heat-resistant platter. Spoon one-half the sauce over asparagus; cover generously with chicken pieces. Fold whipped cream into remaining sauce; pour over chicken. Heat at 350 degrees for 20 minutes. Sprinkle with Parmesan cheese. Place under broiler 5 to 6 inches from heat; broil til brown.

SPAGHETTI CHARLYSS

Add ¾ cup of good-grade, imported olive oil to a non-stick pot. Allow to heat over a medium flame for 2 to 3 minutes. Chop: 2 good-sized onions, ½ cup of parsley, 3 to 4 cups of pre-cooked ham, 1 stalk of celery, 4 good-sized cloves of garlic.

Add the chopped onions to the pot and stir thoroughly, allow to sauté for 2 minutes. Thereafter add the celery and parsley, stirring thoroughly. Allow these ingredients to sauté for about 7 to 10 minutes.

Add the chopped ham, 4 cans of tomato sauce, and stir thoroughly, mixing all the ingredients.

About 10 minutes into the cooking, add 2 tablespoons of grated cheese and stir thoroughly. At this time the addition of 4 or 5 good-sized bay leaves enhances the sauce's flavor.

Now add the finely chopped garlic to the cooking sauce. Allow everything to cook from 45 minutes to an hour, being careful to stir thoroughly every 2 or 3 minutes. After the hour's cooking is done, turn off the fire and let it sit for 10 minutes; then serve over a good-grade, boiled pasta. Serves 3 to 4 people.

ROSE'S SPAGHETTI CASSEROLE

1 ¾ cups raw spaghetti (all broken up)
¼ green pepper, chopped
¼ cup diced pimiento
¼ cup sweet milk
1 ½ – 2 cups cubed turkey, chicken or tuna
½ onion chopped
1 can cream of mushroom soup
½ teaspoon salt
⅛ teaspoon pepper
1 ¾ cups grated rat cheese

Cook your spaghetti and place it in a 2-quart casserole; add remaining ingredients. Bake at 350 degrees for 45 minutes.

"You can make a casserole out of anything. Throw your leftovers into an oven dish and mix with whatever you think will stick them together, an egg or some cheese maybe. Then bake til done." — *Betty Lou Hamilton, Groves, Texas.*

STEWED CHICKEN

2 cans Stokley's tomato sauce
4 bay leaves
2 tablespoons of brown sugar
1 tablespoon white vinegar
1 frying size chicken
1 can water
1 small onion, peeled and chopped
1 green bell pepper
2 tablespoons of oleo

Simmer onions and bell pepper in two tablespoons of oleo. Dump in tomato sauce, water, sugar, vinegar and bay leaves. Let cook slowly for 35 or 40 minutes. Stew chicken in another pan til tender. Pour mixture over drained chicken and simmer for 15 to 20 minutes and serve with rice, corn pone, and combination salad.

This is a coastal chicken stew. An inland one would not have tomatoes, bay leaves, brown sugar or bell peppers. It would be white and thick.

"If you follow the instructions on your pressure cooker you can cook a chicken til the meat falls off the bone in 20 minutes." — *Norma Jean Smith.*

LIVER-HATER'S CHICKEN LIVERS

1 lb. chicken livers   1 small bunch parsley
1 cup sweet sherry   1 cup cracker meal
1 small bunch green onions   salt and pepper

Cut the chicken livers into 1 to 1 ½ inch pieces. Put in a glass bowl. Add salt, pepper and ½ of the sherry, then let 'em soak for 30 minutes to an hour. Now chop your onions (green part and all) and parsley (not the stems) and set them aside.

When your livers are ready, roll them in cracker meal and fry in a hot skillet in ½ inch of grease. Turn them over a lot so they can brown on all sides. Then remove from skillet and pour off grease (but leave the drippins). Put onions and parsley in the skillet and fry for 1 minute. Now return the livers and add sherry. Simmer down for 15 minutes (or until the liquid is almost gone). You're guaranteed to like them even if you hate liver.

AUNT DONNAH'S ROAST POSSUM

Possum should be cleaned as soon as possible after shooting. It should be hung for 48 hours and is then ready to be skinned and cooked. The meat is light-colored and tender. Excess fat may be removed, but there is no strong flavor or odor contained in the fat.

1 possum	1 cup breadcrumbs
1 onion, chopped	1 hard-boiled egg, chopped
1 tablespoon fat	1 teaspoon salt
¼ teaspoon Worcestershire Sauce	water

Rub possum with salt and pepper. Brown onion in fat. Add possum liver and cook until tender. Add breadcrumbs, Worcestershire sauce, egg, salt, and water. Mix thoroughly and stuff possum. Truss like a fowl. Put in roasting pan with bacon across back and pour quart of water into pan. Roast uncovered in moderate oven (350 degrees) until tender, about 2 ½ hours.

There's only one thing to serve possum with — sweet potatoes. You only eat possum in the winter.

RABBIT PIE

Rabbits should be decapitated and dressed immediately after shooting. After skinning, wipe the carcass with a cloth dipped in scalding water to remove loose hair. Cut rabbit into serving pieces. Soak in equal parts of vinegar and water for 12 – 24 hours. Drain and wipe dry. *Sprinkle with salt and pepper and dredge with flour. Sear quickly in frying pan til golden. Add water to cover and simmer slowly in covered pot for 1 ½ hours. Add 2 onions, 2 medium-sized carrots and 2 or 3 potatoes, all cut in pieces. Cook until vegetables are done. Thicken with flour. Cook in a greased baking dish in a hot oven until bubbling. Cover with biscuit dough and return to oven to bake til dough is done.

* *If you're using a bought rabbit, leave off all the soaking and start here.*

FRIED RABBIT

Cut up the rabbit into frying-size pieces. Soak it in vinegar and salt water (enough to cover) for about 1 – 2 hours. Take it out, pat it dry. Salt, pepper, and flour it. Put it in a hot skillet (with enough oil for frying) and fry until a rich brown and, when you stick it with a knife, you don't see any blood. Make gravy with the drippins.

BROILED SQUIRREL

Squirrel is one of the finest and tenderest of all wild meats. Its flavor is mild, rarely gamey. There is no need for soaking, and seldom any need for parboiling. They should be cleaned as soon as possible after shooting, but skinning may wait until they're ready to be cooked.

Clean squirrels and rub with salt and pepper. Brush with fat and place on hot broiling rack. Broil 40 minutes, turning frequently and basting with drippins every 10 minutes. Serve with gravy from drippins and season with 1 to 2 tablespoons of lemon juice.

FRIED SQUIRREL

Make sure all the hair is cleaned off the squirrel. Cut it up. If it's old and tough, put it in the pressure cooker for about 15 – 20 minutes.

Salt and pepper it. Cover with flour and fry in a cast iron skillet on a medium fire until brown and tender. This is a real sweet meat.

You can smother a squirrel just like a chicken.

BUTT'S 'GATOR TAIL

The only place you can find alligator is near the coast or the inland swamps in the South. So if you're lucky enough to get a holt to an alligator tail, there's a section about a foot long just behind the back legs that's tender and juicy. You cut it in sections at the joints just like you would a pork chop. Salt, pepper and flour each piece of tail and then fry in hot grease until golden brown. Or you can barbecue it with Bosie's Barbecue Sauce (page 49). He had alligator tail especially in mind when he concocted it.

If you haven't eaten 'gator tail before, you're in for a surprise. It's gonna taste a little bit like chicken, a little bit like pork, and a little bit like fish. It's so good, you'll wanna lay down and scream.

VENISON ROAST

Take a sharp knife and stick holes in the roast and stuff each hole with a sliver of garlic. The holes should be about 1 ½ – 2 inches apart like a pork roast. Then rub the roast with lots of salt and pepper. Flour it generously. Put in your dutch oven with ⅛ inch grease, and fry til golden brown on all sides. Put on the lid and cook *very slowly* until tender. No vegetables except potatoes, if you want them.

The meat should make its own juice, but if it doesn't, add a touch of white wine. NEVER add water to venison roast.

If you want to soak it overnight, some people do it in milk, some people do it in vinegar and salt water, and some don't do it at all.

MAMMA'S BROWN GRAVY

Leave enough grease in the skillet after frying meat (pork, beef, or chicken) and add 3 or 4 heaping tablespoons of flour on medium-to-high heat and stir constantly with a fork until dark golden brown. Then add water and cook until it just will run out of a spoon. Also, leave the crispies in the grease from the fried meat because they add a lot of rich flavor. Salt and black pepper to taste. Serve over hot rice, grits, or mashed potatoes.

YANKEE CREAM GRAVY

½ cup flour   salt and pepper
1 cup milk

To avoid lumps, put milk and flour in a jar and shake it vigorously until blended. After you have fried some green tomatoes, remove them from the pan and pour in the mixture of flour and milk. Stir constantly until it thickens and serve on top of the green tomatoes.

This will go with just about anything.

RED EYE GRAVY

After cooking the breakfast meat (bacon, ham, or sausage), remove it from the iron skillet and put it aside. To the drippins, pour ⅓ cup of strong coffee and stir while on the fire. Pour over hot grits or sop up with hot biscuits.

BOSIE'S BARBECUE SAUCE

(for all Meats, Fish and Fowl)

½ cup brown sugar
2 lemons
1 cup vinegar
3 cloves garlic
2 tablespoons ketchup
3 tablespoons mustard
   prepared
1 onion (chipped), large
3 strips bacon

2 tablespoons
   Worcestershire sauce
   (optional)
1 cup water
   pepper to taste
½ teaspoon salt
1 dash liquid smoke
   (optional)

Fry bacon until deep gold. Add onions and finish frying until they start getting brown. Add garlic and everything else in the recipe and bring to a boil. Turn fire down and simmer until sauce thickens.

Use on any meat for barbecueing.

(Tip) Rub the meat all over with brown sugar and salt and pepper.

Bosie said: "I smoked a number-three wash tub full of fish last week use'n this very sauce."

Fish, Cooter, 'n Shrimp

PERLOW

This is a rice dish unique to the coasts of North Florida, Georgia and South Carolina. It's like the Jambalaya of Louisiana; anything can be used to make it.

Shrimp Perlow

3 chopped onions
3 chopped toes of garlic
1 cup of chopped ham,
    bacon, or salt meat

oil if needed
1 chopped bell pepper
3 chopped ripe tomatoes
    or 1 can of stewed

Fry down onions, garlic and ham in a black iron pot that has a tight-fitting lid (but don't use it yet). When it's brown, add peppers and tomatoes. Simmer until tomatoes fall apart. Then add salt, pepper, tabasco, a good teaspoon of thyme, and 3 whole bay leaves. Add 2 cups of washed rice and cover with ½ inch of water. Bring to a rolling boil and drop in 2 or 3 lbs. of small, shelled shrimp. Stir them in, put the lid on, turn the fire to low, and cook until the rice is dry and fluffy. This is delicious with cold potato salad, especially if the perlow is peppery hot.

For a white perlow, put in chicken, pork backbones, or sausage with the onions and leave out the tomatoes.

For other good red perlows, use sausage, squirrel or chicken. And remember, shrimp is the only one that you add the meat to after you put in the rice. In the others the meat is put in with the onions to brown.

BETTER BAKED FISH

Soak 2 – 3 lbs. of King mackerel in:

2 tablespoons of ketchup
2 teaspoons of vinegar
1 tablespoon of oil
⅓ teaspoon curry powder

½ teaspoon sweet basil
½ teaspoon sage
    salt and pepper
    dash of garlic powder

After 2 or 3 hours (better overnight), remove fish from sauce and place on tinfoil. Spoon on some of the sauce and add ½ cup of cheap Sauterne. Then wrap tightly in tinfoil and bake at 400 degrees for 20 minutes.

When serving, spoon some of the uncooked sauce onto the hot fish.

FRIED CATFISH FILLET

For about 1 to 3 hours soak your catfish in 2 teaspoons of mustard, 3 or 4 tablespoons of canned cream, plus some salt and pepper.

Roll it in white cornmeal and fry to light golden brown in 1 inch of grease in a hot skillet. Catfish fries fast, so don't overcook it. It should be crispy on the outside and moist on the inside. If you serve it with anything else but hushpuppies, grits, cole slaw, and home fries, it'll get up and walk off the plate.

DAY-OLD FRIED FISH
(Cold & Pickled)

3 bay leaves	¼ cup of white vinegar
1 bunch of green onions chopped, or 1 medium yellow onion chopped	1 lime (use only the juice)
	3 tablespoons of ketchup
2 tablespoons of cooking oil	½ cup of stewed tomatoes salt to taste and pepper (tabasco) to taste
1 large clove of garlic, sliced	left over fried fish

Heat oil in iron pan. Fry green onions and garlic until limp. Add tomatoes and bay leaves and cook 15 minutes. Then add lime juice, ketchup, vinegar, salt and tabasco. Cook another 15 minutes.

Place cold fish in a deep dish in layers, and pour the above ingredients (hot) over the cold fish and let stand in refrigerator from 2 hours to 2 days. The longer you let it stand, the better the flavors.

Be careful of the bones.

SALMON PIE

2 eggs, beaten
1 teaspoon lemon juice
1 tablespoon chopped
    parsley
½ teaspoon pepper
½ cup buttered
    breadcrumbs

½ cup sweet milk
2 teaspoons chopped onion
½ teaspoon sage
1 1 pound can salmon,
    drained

Combine all ingredients in order given; place in 8-inch greased dish. Bake at 350 degrees for 40 minutes.

TUNA SALAD

1 can tuna
1 medium yellow onion
    (grated)
¼ cup hamburger pickles
    (chopped)
2 eggs (hard-boiled and
    chopped)
¼ cup celery (chopped fine)

½ apple, peeled and
    chopped larger than
    celery
black pepper
salt, if you think it
    needs it
½ – 1 cup mayonnaise

Mix all together and serve on toasted bread, or eat it on crackers. Good by itself, too!

FRIDAY'S TUNA FISH SALAD

1 can of tuna fish
½ medium yellow onion
    (finely chopped)
3 tablespoons of pickle
    relish

⅓ cup of mayonnaise
3 hard-boiled eggs
    (chopped up)
salt and pepper

Open your can of tuna fish. Turn it upside down (with the loose lid still on) and drain all the liquid out of the can. Dump it in a bowl. Add everything else and salt and pepper to taste.

If it's not juicy enough for you, add more mayonnaise. Serve on a leaf of lettuce or make sandwiches out of the bowl.

There's nothing better with tuna fish salad than potato chips, so make sure you've got a big bag for the folks.

FOUR-CAN DEEP TUNA PIE

1 can French-style green beans, drained	1 medium-sized can tuna
1 can of Campbell's mushroom soup	½ can of milk
1 tablespoon of oleo	1 can of French-Fried onion rings, or a box of frozen

Dilute soup with milk. Stir together beans, tuna, and soup. Bake at 400 degrees until bubbly. Top with onion rings. Put it back in the oven just long enough to make onion rings crispy. Serves 6.

CLARA JANE VICKAR'S CREAMED TUNA LUNCH

Brown 2 tablespoons of flour and 3 tablespoons of butter or oleo in a skillet. Add the tuna (big can is best) chunk style and 1 small container half-and-half or 2 cups of milk. Cook over low heat til thickened. Salt, pepper, and serve with toast or rice. Carnation evaporated milk is good in this, too.

COOTER PIE

1 medium-sized cooter	2 slices toasted bread
½ cup stewed tomatoes	(crumbled)
1 cup sweet milk	Worcestershire sauce
1 cup liquor from stew pot	2 tablespoons oleo
1 tablespoon whiskey	1 tablespoon sherry
celery salt	mace
red pepper	black pepper to taste
2 hard-boiled eggs, cut up	

Drop live cooter in a pot of boiling water. Cook 45 minutes. Open shell with a saw and take out meat, fat, liver, and eggs. Be careful not to break the gall. Remove meat from the feet and legs. Put all this in a pot with a little water and salt. Then stew until tender, usually about one hour. Next, cut up meat, liver, and eggs. Add stewed tomatoes, milk, liquor from stew pot, oleo, whiskey, sherry, eggs (cut up), breadcrumbs and seasonings. Put in shell (which has been provided by the cooter and has been thoroughly cleaned). Cover with cracker crumbs, dot with oleo, and bake in 375-degree oven about 45 minutes.

MOCK COOTER SOUP

3 pounds lean beef or	1½ quarts of water
ground meat	¼ pound of oleo
1 pint sweet milk	½ pint cream
1 tablespoon flour	2 hard-boiled eggs cut up
½ teaspoon mace	in medium-size chunks
½ teaspoon dry mustard	

Boil meat and water until one quart of liquid remains. Add one pint of milk and ¼ pound oleo. Remove meat, allow to cool, grind, and return to stock. Let it cook down a little more. Add flour dissolved in cream. Add seasoning.

Miz Ina also says: "To make a real one just add cooter meat instead of ground meat. That's the way we do it in Sandfly, Georgia."

MISSISSIPPI SHRIMP SUPREME

2 pounds shrimp	4 tablespoons flour
1 bay leaf	8 tablespoons tomato
red pepper (dash)	ketchup
½ lemon (the juice)	1 – 1½ cups milk
salt and pepper to taste	4 tablespoons
4 tablespoons oleo	Worcestershire sauce

Cream oleo and flour. Add milk and make a thick cream sauce. Add Worcestershire sauce, ketchup, bay leaf, red pepper and lemon juice. Salt and pepper to taste. Add cooked shrimp and allow to get very hot. Serve in a ring of rice.

Rayette said she picked the recipe up at some fancy restaurant while she was on vacation at Shell Beach, Miss.

MRS. ARNOLD'S SATURDAY NIGHT SHRIMPS

In a big piece of cheesecloth, tie up 3 bay leaves, 2 cloves of garlic, one minced onion for each pound of shrimp, 2 lemons (sliced), and 2 dried peppers. Boil shrimp spices in a big pot of water for 15 minutes. Dump unpeeled (but headed) shrimp in, and boil them for ten minutes. Then remove the shrimp and set aside. Pour out half the water in the pot, remove spice bag, and add juice from a large jar of Heinz's sweet pickles. Then, cook the liquid down some more. Return the shrimp to this juice and chill for about 4 hours. Drain. Serve with the sweet pickles left from the juice, crackers, and ketchup. Let everybody peel their own.

SHRIMP AND EGGPLANT CASSEROLE

2 eggplants
1 medium onion, chopped
1 medium bell pepper,
   chopped
1 cup celery, chopped fine
   red pepper, paprika,
   garlic, salt
2 lbs. shrimp

2 cups slightly undercooked
   rice (measure after
   cooked)
1 can buttered, toasted
   crumbs
½ lb. sharp cheddar cheese,
   grated
¼ cup vegetable oil

In a heavy iron skillet over a medium fire, fry shrimp in the oil, stirring lightly until they are pink. Remove shrimp from skillet and fry onions, celery, and bell pepper until tender but still crisp. Add to shrimp.

Peel eggplant, cut in cubes, cover with slightly-salted water, and let simmer until tender, but not too soft. Drain well, add salt and pepper, then mix rice, eggplant and shrimp mixture. It should be highly seasoned (pepper). Stir lightly and spoon into a 2½ quart buttered casserole. Pour undiluted can of cream of mushroom soup over top of mixture, then grated cheese. Lastly, add the buttered, toasted breadcrumbs. Sprinkle with paprika, place in pre-heated, 350-degree oven for 25 minutes. Serves 8.

This recipe is from the table of Father Bob Landry, St. Alphonse Catholic Church, Maurice, La. He always says "They got more, cher!"

CRAB STEW OR CLAM CHOWDER

3 tablespoons of bacon fat
2 large onions (chopped)
3 toes of garlic (sliced)
1 large can of stewed
   tomatoes or 2 cups of
   home-stewed
3 bay leaves

4 – 5 medium potatoes
   (cut up)
1 dozen fresh crabs (still
   wiggling), or frozen
1 cup of crab meat
1 teaspoon of thyme
   salt and pepper to taste

Put onions, garlic, and bacon fat into a hot skillet and fry until golden. Add the tomatoes, juice and all, and cook it down until all the liquid is gone. Pour this into a stew pot and add the potatoes, bay leaves and hot peppers. Cover with the water, add salt and pepper and simmer on medium fire until the potatoes are tender.

Meanwhile take the shells off the crabs and remove the devils fingers (the pointed things). Do not remove the legs. Now, chop the bodies in half and crack the claws with the handle of the knife. When the potatoes are tender, tump the crabs (bodies and claws) and the crab meat into the stew. Add thyme and more water if needed. Cook twenty more minutes and serve over rice.

You can thicken this with ½ cup of skillet-browned flour (dry) right after you put the crab meat in.

Clam Chowder: It's exactly the same except use clams instead of crabs. It takes 3 cups clam meat, fresh or canned (chopped).

SHEBA SPANN'S SHE-CRAB SOUP

1 tablespoon oleo	1 teaspoon flour
1 quart sweet milk	2 cups white crab meat
¼ pint cream whipped	and crab eggs
few drops onion juice	½ teaspoon salt
⅛ teaspoon mace	⅛ teaspoon pepper
4 tablespoons dry sherry	
½ teaspoon Worcestershire	
sauce	

Melt the oleo in top of a double boiler and blend with flour until smooth. Add the milk gradually, stirring constantly. To this add crab meat and eggs and all seasonings except sherry. Cook slowly over hot water for 20 minutes. To serve, place a tablespoon of warmed sherry in individual soup bowls, then add soup and top with whipped cream. Sprinkle with paprika or finely chopped parsley.

Secret: If unable to obtain "She-crabs", crumble yolk of hard-boiled eggs in bottom of soup plates.

Sheba Spann says: "You can fool the best of 'em!"

KLEBERT'S COLD CRAWFISH SOUP

1 medium onion	2 cups milk
2 tablespoons butter	1 cup thick cream
2 white potatoes	tabasco, celery salt, and
2 cups chicken broth	pepper, to taste
1½ teaspoons salt	1 – 2 lbs. crawfish tails

Mais cher, if you don't stay to South Louisiana, you fish market probably won't have crawfish, mais shrimp will do.

Brown you onions in butter; add you potatoes (sliced thin), broth, and salt. Bring to boil, cover and simmer for thirty minutes. Puree in you 'lectric mixer and then add you cream and season. Add half you crawfish or shrimp and puree again. Add you other crawfish tails or shrimp whole and cool in you ice box 'til real cold. Serves 6 – 8 of you best hungry friends.

Dinner Salads
'n Sweet Salads

COMBINATION SALAD

1 head iceberg lettuce   3 medium-size tomatoes
                                    (ripe)

Rinse your lettuce and chop into 2-inch pieces (bite-size). Clean your tomatoes and cut them up into 1-inch squares.

Combine the tomatoes, lettuce and enough mayonnaise to generously coat everything. Then salt and black pepper to taste and tumble some more. If more moisture is needed, add a spoon or two of white vinegar.

"It's so good with fried chicken or pork chops and is enough to feed a whole family," says Betty Sue, "and there ain't no secret to makin' it."

LAURA LEE'S FRESH SUMMER SALAD

2 cucumbers   2 medium-sized tomatoes
                                    (ripe)

Take your cucumber and cut off the ends. Then with an end in one hand, the cucumber in the other, rub together real hard and fast. When the liquid starts to foam, stop. Now peel and slice them.

Meanwhile, slice your tomatoes and place both the cucumbers and tomatoes in a long, low, Pyrex baking dish, and cover with cider vinegar, and salt and pepper to taste. Chill for ½ hour before serving. Delicious with field peas or black-eyed peas.

HAM-LIMA SALAD

Chop your four hard-boiled eggs. Cut two cups of ham into ½-inch cubes. Add two cups of drained, cooked green lima beans, one cup of chopped celery, 1 tablespoon finely chopped onion, ½ cup Blue Plate mayonnaise, ½ teaspoon curry powder, salt and pepper. Mix, taste for salt, chill an hour or more to blend flavors. Then help your plate!

MONA LISA SAPP'S MACARONI SALAD

4 cups of elbow macaroni
(cooked and drained)
½ cup mayo
3 – 4 tablespoons sweet
pickle relish
¼ cup onion
(finely chopped)

1 small jar of pimientos
(chopped)
2 tablespoons light
salad oil
1 teaspoon French's
mustard
salt and pepper to taste

Put everything together in a big bowl and mix it very good. If you need more juice, add a spoon or 2 of vinegar and re-mix. This goes very well with fried foods (hot or cold). It's enough for a tableful.

To this recipe you can add either 1 cup of cubed cheese, 1 can flaked tuna, 1 cup fried ground meat (cold), or 1 cup of chicken meat (cooked and chopped).

Mona says: "You can turn this salad everyway but loose and it's gonna be good!"

REBECCA VENERABLE'S SAUERKRAUT SALAD

1 large can sauerkraut
1 onion (medium)
1 green pepper
½ cup celery

jar pimientos
½ cup vinegar
½ cup olive oil
1 cup sugar

Chop onion, pepper, celery, pimientos, and also chop sauerkraut. Mix all ingredients together and let stand two days before eating.

RICE SALAD

2 cups cooked, chilled rice
½ cup chopped king crab
    or lobster
½ cup slivered Virginia ham
½ cup finely chopped celery
2 finely chopped
    hard-boiled eggs
    salt and freshly ground
    pepper

1 tablespoon chopped
    chives
¼ cup chopped parsley
1 tablespoon olive oil
1 tablespoon wine vinegar
½ cup Blue Plate
    mayonnaise

Combine by tossing lightly the rice, crab, ham, celery, eggs, chives, and parsley. Sprinkle with oil and vinegar. Add mayonnaise and season. Let stand in the ice box for a few hours for still better flavor.

AUNT CORA'S COLESLAW

1 medium head of
    cabbage
1 medium yellow onion
    (chopped)
½ pint of mayonnaise (use
    more if you want it
    juicy)

3 heaping tablespoons of
    pickle relish (a little
    juice)
    salt and pepper

Shred and chop that cabbage head until it's as fine as you like it, and then put it in a bowl. To the bowl, add your onion, mayonnaise, pickle relish, salt and pepper to taste. (Black pepper is very important to a good coleslaw.) Now let it stand in the ice box for 2 or 3 hours before using.

    This is perfect for a big fish fry with hush puppies, home fries, and grits. (Page 54).

ANGEL FLAKE AMBROSIA

6 – 8 oranges (peeled and cut up)
4 – 5 bananas (cut into rounds)
1 bag Angel Flake coconut

1 medium-size jar of maraschino cherries (with juice, cut in half)
1 – 2 cups of sugar to taste .

Mix all the fruit together and add sugar, cherries, and coconut. Put in the refrigerator and serve ice cold. It should be good and juicy. Christmas wouldn't be Christmas without it, and it's even better if you let it set til New Year's.

SURPRISE SALAD

½ cup cold water
3 envelopes plain gelatin
5 cups applesauce (2 No. 2 cans)

¼ cup red cinammon candy
½ cup white sugar
½ teaspoon nutmeg
2 tablespoons lemon juice

Put your gelatin in a bowl; add your cold water and dissolve it. Heat candy and applesauce in a pan on medium heat until it bubbles. Then you add your gelatin. Then add all the other ingredients. Then pour the mixture into a mayonnaised mold. Now you chill it til it's firm; and then you unmold it and garnish with parsley or anything green.

"Even Reba get jealous when I make this," says Stella Carlisle of Eclectic, Alabama.

FANNIE'S FIVE-CUP SALAD

1 cup of little
    marshmallows (white,
    not colored)
1 cup of Angel Flake
    coconut

1 cup of canned mandarin
    oranges (drained)
1 cup Libby's fruit
    cocktail (drained)
1 cup of sour cream

Combine all these ingredients in a large glass or Tupperware bowl. Cover; place in the ice box for two hours or overnight. May be served as a salad or dessert. Nuts and cherries (canned) may be added.

Mrs. Fannie Paulk, of Evening Shade, Ark., says: "It'll dress up any occasion, it's so fancy!"

FRUITED SOUR CREAM SALAD (BANANAS)

6 bananas (firm and not
    too ripe)
1 pint of sour cream or
    imitation

1 cup of brown sugar
1 teaspoon of cinnamon
1 can of mandarin oranges
½ teaspoon of nutmeg

Slice bananas and add drained mandarin oranges in a bowl. Mix sour cream, sugar, cinnamon, and nutmeg. Pour over bananas and oranges. Mix and chill.

FRUITED SOUR CREAM SALAD (WHITE GRAPES)

2 lbs. seedless white grapes
1 pint of sour cream or
    imitation

1 cup brown sugar
1 teaspoon cinnamon
½ teaspoon of nutmeg

Wash grapes and pick from stems. Mix sour cream, sugar, cinnamon, and nutmeg. Pour over grapes and chill. (You can cut your grapes in half if you want to.)

Jinny Beaufort Houseworth says: "These are both flavorites at every brunch in Ty Ty, Georgia!"

For brunch these are delicious with scrambled eggs, grits and sausage.

LUCY'S GUARANTEED STEWED PRUNES

1 lb. box of prunes
½ cup of sugar

1 lemon (sliced)

Dump your prunes in a pot and cover with cold water. Put them on the fire and bring to a slow and easy boil for 15 minutes.

Now add your sugar and lemon and cook for 15 minutes more. Remove from the fire and cool. Serves 8.

Delicious with cheese dishes, and good for you too.

Sandwiches 'n Eggs

KISS ME NOT SANDWICH

Spread mustard on two pieces of bread. Then slice onion on one and cover with the other. Ice tea helps wash it down.

ANOTHER KISS ME NOT SANDWICH

2 slices of bread   peanut butter
  (wholewheat)   sliced bermuda onion

Spread on the peanut butter and place on the slices of onion. Put them together and eat. You'll need a drink with this.

CANNED CORN BEEF SANDWICH

Butter two pieces of bread with mayonnaise (generously). Cover one with sliced corn beef and bread 'n butter pickles. Top with the other piece of bread. This is delicious with a Cocola!

ANTI-STICK PEANUT BUTTER SANDWICH

Butter one slice of bread with peanut butter, then butter the other side with mayonnaise (generously). Put them together and eat (will not stick to roof of your mouth — partials not included).
    Delicious with glass of cold milk.

POTATO CHIP SANDWICH

2 slices of bread   potato chips
  mayonnaise

Spread the mayo generously across the bread. Pile the potato chips on to one of the slices as high as you can. Then top it with the other slice and mash down until all the potato chips are crushed.

Pardie Tickette says: "Wash it down with a Pepsi, it's some good!"

PAPER-THIN GRILL CHEESE

2 slices of Velveeta cheese   2 slices of white bread
  (no other will do)   (no other will do)

Heat your iron skillet with a pat or two of butter in the bottom. Put your slices of Velveeta cheese between the 2 slices of bread. Now place it in the hot skillet. With a turner, mash and toast the cheese sandwich on both sides until the cheese is melted and the bread is toasted. (The flatter the better.)

KITCHEN SINK TOMATO SANDWICH

In the peak of the tomato season, chill 1 very large or 2 medium tomatoes that have been vine-ripened and have a good acidy bite to their taste.

Take two slices of bread. Coat them with ¼ inch of good mayonnaise. On one piece of bread, slice the tomato ¼ inch thick. Salt and pepper that layer. Add another layer of sliced tomato, and again salt and pepper. Place the other piece of bread on top of this, roll up your sleeves, and commence to eat over the kitchen sink while the juice runs down your elbows.

FRIED EGG SANDWICH

Spread two slices of bread with mayonnaise. Put the fried egg (soft or hard) between them after you've salted and peppered it.

Sometimes this is the only way you can eat breakfast.

CHARLOTTE'S DEVILED EGGS

You hard-boil your eggs, cut 'em in half, longwise, and then take the yellow and toss it out. Throw in some Hellman's mayonnaise, pickle juice, lemon juice, celery salt, and celery seed (that's the secret). Mash all this up well and then stuff it back into the whites; and, if you want to be fancy, put a dash of red or black caviar on top.

RICE AND EGGS

1 cup used rice	salt to taste
5 eggs	pepper to taste
⅓ cup milk, cream, or sour cream	1 squirt of tabasco

Beat eggs, milk, salt, and pepper. Pour in medium-hot greased skillet. Stir til eggs start lumping together, then add rice. Cook until they're the way you like them. Serves 3 or 4.

"When you're scramblin eggs, always add a little milk or cream to make them lighter and go further," says Barbara Jean Hubbard, Mill Creek, Alabama.

IDA'S INDIAN ONION CURRY OMELET

1 tablespoon of vegetable
   oil
6 – 7 eggs
3 green scallions
1 teaspoon of curry powder

1 teaspoon prepared
   mustard (French's
   yellow)
½ cup of milk

Fry sliced green onions in medium-hot skillet. Add mixture of eggs, milk, curry, mustard, and salt and pepper to taste. Cook until eggs are firm and all liquid is gone. Serves 4 or 5.

Serve with toast and plain sardines, cold.

Ida Dillard, of Due West, South Carolina, said: "You got to be kinda wild to try this one. It weeds 'em out."

LEETTA'S FANCY EGGS & CHEESE PIE

4 whole eggs
1 cup of chopped parsley
1 cup of Swiss cheese,
   grated

½ teaspoon of nutmeg
½ pint of whipping cream
1 unbaked 9-inch pie shell

Mix eggs, cream, nutmeg, salt, and pepper. Pour into pie shell that has been baked for 5 minutes at 400 degrees. Sprinkle in cheese and parsley and bake for 25 minutes at 350 degrees or until brown on top.

Mrs De Wald says: "This ain't our dessert, it's for a light supper or brunch."

OOZIE'S OKRA OMELET

1 cup of fresh okra, cut
   in rounds
½ cup chopped scallions

6 – 7 eggs
⅓ cup of milk

Fry okra and onions in 2 tablespoons of bacon grease or oil til onions are clear and okra is bright green.

Remove okra and onions. Stir eggs into the skillet til they start thickening; then add okra and onion and work til done. 5 – 9 minutes. Serves 4 to 5.

Best with cornbread.

(See: CORNBREAD)

CHEESE EGGS

¾ cups of cheese (your choice, but it was always done with Velveeta)	6 – 7 eggs ⅓ cup of milk 2 squirts of tabasco sauce salt and pepper to taste

Beat eggs, milk, salt, pepper and tabasco sauce. Pour into hot, greased skillet. Stir til eggs start lumping. Add cheese. Stir til done. Serves 4 or 6.

Serve with hot biscuits filled with sliced bananas and topped with mayonnaise.

MOTHER'S MARBLE EGGS

½ cup grated Swiss cheese ½ cup chopped green onions	6 eggs ½ stick of butter or margarine

Fry onions in margarine til limp. Break eggs in skillet as if cooking them sunny side up without breaking the yolks. Stir whites and onions around the yolks being careful not to break them yet. When the whites are firm *break* the yolks and add cheese and stir everything together. Then serve immediately.

ALMA'S ALMOND OMELET

½ cup slivered almonds   6 eggs
½ stick margarine or butter

Brown almonds in margarine in skillet (medium heat) until toasted. Beat eggs in bowl and add to almonds. Stir until eggs are firm. Salt and pepper to taste. Serves 3 or 4.

GIRL SCOUT ONE-EYED EGG

1 slice of bread (loaf   1 egg
    style, your choice)

With a glass, cut a circle from the center of the slice of bread and remove circle to the side. Heat greased skillet and put slice of bread in it. Brown one side, then turn. Then break egg shell and put egg in hole in center of bread being careful not to break the yellow. Cook to taste and serve with bacon or sausage and toasted round (the one removed). Serves 1.

MRS. ARNOLD'S DAUGHTER MARTHA'S EGG; OR, "A MARTHA EGG"

Beat an egg with ¼ cup of milk, a pinch of salt and pepper. Fry in butter at a low heat. Serve with a sweet smile and a kind word. If serving to a kid, pat it on the head. This egg is pure love and heals all wounds.

CUCUMBER EGGS

1 small cucumber, sliced
6 – 7 eggs
2 scallions or 2 tablespoons
   of chopped onion
⅓ cup of milk, cream,
   or sour cream

1 squirt of tabasco or
   Worcestershire sauce
salt and pepper to taste
1 big dash of curry powder

Fry onion and cucumber til limp and you can see through them. Remove from skillet.

Add beaten eggs, salt, pepper, and sauce to hot skillet. When eggs are lumping, add cucumber and onions. Stir til it's medium soft, or hard, or whatever you like. Serves 4 or 6.

Good with hot sardines and mustard.

Betty Sue told me: "You can throw anything into an egg and it'll come out good!"

PEGGY'S PIG EGGS

6 hard-boiled eggs (peeled)
2 eggs, beaten
1 lb. of loose sausage meat

1 cup of breadcrumbs or
   cornmeal

Mix ½ the beaten eggs with the sausage meat. Pat the meat around the outside of the boiled eggs until it's even all the way round. then smear the rest of the beaten eggs on the meat-covered eggs and roll them in the breadcrumbs. Now you should have something that looks like 6 large goose eggs. Fry these in a heavy iron skillet with ½ inch of oil in the bottom until golden brown. Make sure you roll them round while they're frying so as to brown them evenly. Drain on a brown paper bag to get rid of the extra grease, and then chill them overnight before using. "Your company won't believe their eyes when they cut them open," says Peggy Lou Dawson of Pee Dee, North Carolina.

Candies, Cakes, Cobblers 'n Cookies

GERDIE'S GROUNDNUT CANDY

1 quart molasses
4 cups shelled peanuts,
   roasted

1 cup brown sugar
½ cup oleo

Combine all ingredients except nuts, and boil for one-half hour over a slow fire. Then add the roasted and shelled peanuts and continue cooking for fifteen minutes. Drop on lightly greased cookie sheet or on a piece of marble. Make little cakes of the candy and let harden. For peanuts you may substitute benne seed.

B'ANNA'S CRYSTALLIZED GRAPEFRUIT PEEL

Cover grapefruit rinds with cold water and bring to a boil. Pour off water. Repeat this process until there have been 3 boilings.

Cut the rinds, now soft, into any desired shape. Add 1 ½ cups sugar to each grapefruit, but no water.

Stir over the fire for 15 or 20 minutes. This requires hard stirring and careful watching until crystallized. Then roll in sugar.

Color with food color. Delicious and pretty for the tea table.

MAMMA TWO'S PRALINES

2 cups sugar (light brown
   if possible)
2 cups granulated sugar
1 small can evaporated
   milk
1 cup water

2 tablespoons white syrup
½ teaspoon soda
2 teaspoons vanilla
2 tablespoons butter
1 cup pecans (whole)

Blend together milk, water, soda, and syrup. Blend well or milk will curdle. Stir in mixed brown and white sugar. Cook to soft ball stage. Remove from fire and beat until light brown. Put in vanilla, then butter and, last, pecans.

Drop on wax paper and let cool. Makes about 24 good-size patties.

MAMMA'S GONE FUDGE

4 cups of sugar	3 tablespoons of butter
¾ cup water	1 teaspoon vanilla extract
¾ cup canned cream	1½ cups of chopped nuts
½ cup of cocoa	pinch of salt

Bring everything except vanilla, nuts and salt to a boil without stirring and continue until the mixture forms medium-hard balls when dropped in a glass of cold water. Take it off the fire and let it sit without messing with it until it's lukewarm. Now mix in vanilla extract, nuts, and salt.

Beat this until it gets dull looking, then quickly pour into a flat buttered pan and cut into squares before it gets too hard.

For peanut-butter fudge, leave out the cocoa and chopped nuts and put in ½ cup peanut butter.

HOMEMADE FUDGE ICING

2 cups plain sugar	1 box of powdered sugar
2 heaping tablespoons	(sifted)
Hershey's cocoa	1 teaspoon pure vanilla
1 stick oleo	1 pinch of salt
pure evaporated milk	

Stir everything together in a bowl except the powdered sugar and vanilla, and don't add too much milk — just enough to make a good stirring mixture. Put it on the stove and bring to a boil. (Stir it a lot to keep it from sticking.) Take it off the stove and add the powdered sugar, ⅓ at a time. Use your mix-master on this if you're lucky enough to have one. Put in your vanilla and continue beating until the icing is smooth and spreads easily without running. (There's nothing worse than runny icing.)

For caramel icing, use brown sugar instead of white, and leave out the cocoa. For white icing, omit cocoa.

That's three kinds of icing right there.

OLD-FASHIONED POUND CAKE

1 lb. of butter (nothing else will do)	9 eggs
1 lb. of sugar	½ teaspoon cream of tartar
	½ teaspoon salt

Mix first three ingredients at room temperature. Then add 1 teaspoon vanilla extract, 2 or 3 drops of lemon extract, and make sure you stir everything after adding. Now sift 4 cups of cake flour; do it again, and add cream of tartar and salt.

Slowly add the flour to the mixture and make sure you blend it as you go along. Now beat until the batter is smooth and you can't see any lumps. Pour it into a well-greased-and-floured tube pan and bake at 300 degrees for 1 hour. The *secret* to a good pound cake is to make sure you get all the lumps out.

On a plate (bottom covered with rum) put 1 slice of pound cake with 2 big spoons of ice cream (choice of flavor — recipe follows) and 1 more slice of pound cake on top.

Drench in chocolate syrup, and top with fresh whipped cream.

OUR LORD'S SCRIPTURE CAKE

4½ cups (1st Kings 4:22)	flour
1 cup (Judges 5:25, last clause)	butter
2 cups (Jeremiah 6:20)	sugar
2 cups (1st Samuel 30:12)	raisins
2 cups (Nahum 3:12)	figs
2 cups (Numbers 17:18)	almonds
2 tablespoons (1st Samuel 14:13)	honey
1 pinch (Leviticus 2:13)	salt
6 (Jeremiah 17:11)	eggs
½ cup (Judges 4:19, last clause)	milk
2 tablespoons (Amos 4:5)	leaven

Season to taste with (2nd Chronicles 9:9) spices. Mix like a fruit cake and bake.

RESURRECTION CAKE

Take one cake mix, your choice. Mix as directed on box. Pour in a well-greased cake pan, kind of deep. Over the top, pour a pint of stewed pears or other fruit of your choice. Can fruit will do fine, but home-canned is best.

Then cover the top of the fruit with pats of oleo, or butter, and sprinkle with a good coat of sugar.

Stick in pre-heated oven 350 degrees for 30 – 40 minutes, or until cake has risen to hide the fruit and is brown. Eat hot with a good strong whiskey sauce.

WHISKEY SAUCE

2 cups of sugar	1 cup of Jack Daniels
½ lb. of butter (2 sticks)	Black Label
1 teaspoon pure vanilla	1 pinch of salt

Blend sugar and butter and vanilla until mixed completely. Then add whiskey bit by bit, mixing until it is a nice, loose, creamy sauce. The sugar is supposed to be grainy.

Pour over resurrection cake and it's guaranteed to resurrect.

MAMMY'S DATE CAKE

1 cup sugar	½ teaspoon salt
½ cup Wesson oil	1 tablespoon vanilla
4 eggs (whites beaten separately)	1½ – 2 pounds dates
1 cup flour	1 quart shelled pecans, chopped
1 teaspoon baking powder	

Cream sugar, Wesson oil and egg yolks until fluffy. Mix nuts and dates with ½ cup of flour. Add 1 teaspoon baking powder to the other ½ cup of flour. Add salt and combine with creamed yolk mixture. Add flour, nuts, dates, and mix well. Add beaten egg whites and vanilla extract. Mixture will be stiff as a board. Do not moisten. Will have to mix with hands. Place in tube or loaf pan (greased). Bake at 300 until done (brown). If you're not sure, test it with a broom straw, and don't go any further.

MAMMY'S FRUIT CAKE

5 large eggs	¾ lb. glazed cherries
½ lb. butter (not oleo)	1 lb. glazed pineapple
1 cup white sugar	4 cups shelled pecans
1¾ cups flour (not cake	(chopped)
flour)	½ oz. vanilla extract
½ teaspoon baking powder	½ oz. lemon extract

Cream butter and sugar until fluffy. Add well-beaten eggs and blend well. Chop nuts and fruit and mix with part of the flour. Sift remaining flour and baking powder, then fold into egg-and-butter mixture. Add flavorings and mix well. Then add fruit and nuts. Mix thoroughly (by hand). Put mixture in a greased tube pan and place in a cold oven and bake for three hours at 275 degrees. Then let it stand til it's cool and it'll come out real easy.

Mammy's cakes are so heavy the post office won't take them.

GRAND CANYON CAKE

2 boxes of plain white	1 cup of whiskey sauce
cake mix	(page 86)
2 cans of chocolate icing	

Mix cake mixes like they tell you on the box. Then divide each cake mix into half and color each one of the four layers in a different color, such as red, yellow, green, and blue. Then bake them separately in 8-inch cake pans until done. Cool them off before you start to put the icing on. Now put a layer of cake and a layer of icing until you've used up all the cake. You should have enough to cover it generously; if not, run to the store and buy another can. After it's covered, take 2 big forks and stick them in the middle of the top of the cake and force on it until it cracks open and you can see all the colored layers. Now pour your whiskey sauce into the crack and let the cake absorb it. Let it stand for 3 or 4 hours before serving.

This is a wonderful treat for someone that's going to, or just got back from vacationing at, the Grand Canyon. It's also very educational for children.

POTATO CHOCOLATE CAKE

1 cup hot mashed potatoes (unseasoned)
2 cups sugar
⅔ cup Crisco
4 eggs, unbeaten
½ cup milk
2 cups sifted, all-purpose flour
1 cup chopped nuts
3 tablespoons Calumet baking powder
1 tablespoon each of cinnamon and nutmeg
½ tablespoon salt
1 tablespoon vanilla
¾ cup Hershey's cocoa

Prepare mashed potatoes. Gradually beat sugar into Crisco until fluffy. Add eggs one at a time, beating well. Add vanilla and potatoes, and then add sifted ingredients and milk alternately, about ¼ of each at a time, beating smooth. Add nuts. Bake at 350 degrees 40 – 50 minutes.

IRMA LEE STRATTON'S CHOCOLATE DUMP CAKE

3½ cups sifted cake flour
2½ teaspoons Calumet double-action baking powder
1 teaspoon salt
4 eggs
3 cups sugar
¾ cup Hershey's cocoa
1⅓ cups oleo or Crisco
2 cups buttermilk
2 teaspoons McCormick's vanilla extract

Measure and sift together the dry ingredients. Add oleo or Crisco (softened to room temperature) and mix with hands. Then, add buttermilk and beat for 2 minutes. Add eggs and beat again for 2 minutes. Add vanilla. Grease and dust with flour two 10-inch square layer cake pans that are 2 inches deep. Divide cake batter in pans and bake at 350 degrees for one hour.

Stick cakes together with chocolate icing (page 84) and cover with the rest.

1-2-3-4 CAKE

1 cup oleo
2 cups white sugar
3 cups flour
4 eggs
1 scant cup milk or water
2½ teaspoons Calumet
   baking powder

½ teaspoon each of
   McCormick's lemon
   and vanilla extract
   pinch salt

Cream oleo, sugar, and egg yolks. Sift baking powder, salt, and flour together. Add alternately with liquid; add flavorings. Fold in stiffly-beaten whites last. Bake in tube pan at 300 degrees 1¼ hours or until a toothpick inserted comes out clean.

REBA'S RAINBOW ICE-BOX CAKE

1 cup confectioner's sugar
2 egg yolks
1 cup pecans
2 boxes cherry Jello
½ cup oleo

1 No. 2 can Dole crushed
   pineapple
2 boxes lime Jello
1 box (medium size)
   Graham crackers

Cream your sugar, oleo, and egg yolks, and then add your strained pineapple and nuts. Beat your egg whites stiff and fold them in. Then place a layer of Graham crackers on the bottom of a pan, pour in the mixture, and put in the ice box to chill.

Now fix your cherry Jello as for regular use, except use pineapple juice for one cup of water and the other just plain water. Don't pour this mixture over the other mixture in the ice box until it's ready to congeal.

Next fix your lime Jello and let set in the ice box until ready to congeal. Then whip with the egg beater until fluffy and spread it over the pan of mixtures. After this has all congealed, whip one half pint of cream and cover the whole thing.

Slice and serve topped with cherries if you got 'em; if you don't, don't. Reba says you can put as many layers of Graham crackers as you like. Serves about 15. Excellent for Tupperware parties.

SHORT'NIN BREAD

1 ½ cups flour   ¼ cup light brown sugar
¼ pound oleo (soft)

Cream the oleo and sugar. Add the flour and mix thoroughly. Roll out quickly, about ½ inch thick, on a floured board. Use the lid to a fruit jar or a jelly glass to cut out your shapes. Place on greased-and-floured shallow pan and bake at 350 degrees for about 20 minutes.

SOUTHERN SPICY GINGERBREAD

2 eggs   2 teaspoons soda
¾ cup brown sugar   2 teaspoons ginger
¾ cup dark molasses   1 ½ teaspoons cinnamon
¾ cup Crisco   ½ teaspoon ground cloves
2 ½ cups flour   ½ teaspoon Calumet baking
½ teaspoon nutmeg   powder
1 cup boiling water

Add beaten eggs to sugar, molasses, and melted Crisco, and stir good. Add dry ingredients which have been mixed and sifted; and then add the boiling water. Bake in small individual pans or one big shallow pan (make sure you grease them) in moderate oven 350 degrees for 30 or 40 minutes. Serve with lemon sauce.

Basic Lemon Sauce

½ cup sugar
1 tablespoon cornstarch
1 cup water
2 tablespoons of butter
½ teaspoon grated lemon
    rind

3 tablespoons of lemon
    juice (or Real Lemon
    lemon juice)
1 pinch of salt

Combine sugar, cornstarch and water in a pot and cook on high fire until thick. Remove and add the rest of the ingredients. Return it to the fire until it's thick again (about 2 or 3 minutes). Use it while it's hot.

COBBLER

3 cups of cooked or canned
    fruit (apples, peaches,
    blackberries, and so
    on)

⅔ cup of sugar

Use Oleta Brown's pie crust recipe, but add 2 tablespoons of sugar in the flour mixture. You may need 2 portions of this recipe found on page 111.

Next, add the sugar to the fruit and heat, but do not boil it. Then roll out dough. Cut half of it into strips and add them to a 8″ x 8″ pan that's good and greasy. Pour on the fruit and spread evenly all over the top. Poke holes in it with a knife or fork, dot with lots of butter, and sprinkle with cinnamon. Bake it all in 400 degree oven for ½ hour. It's delicious with ice cream in the summer or whiskey sauce (page 86) in the winter.

BASIC ICE CREAM

1 large can evaporated milk
2 quarts whole milk
4 eggs

2 cups white sugar
2 teaspoons McCormick's vanilla extract

Beat eggs, and add sugar and evaporated milk, the whole milk, and vanilla. Put mixture in ice cream churn and churn it until stiff. Now, add 2 cups crushed fruit, if you want to, and then churn it some more until it gets stiff again.

FANNY'S FRUIT-COCKTAIL COBBLER

1 box yellow Betty Crocker cake mix
2 cans fruit cocktail (No. 2½)

2 sticks oleo

Pour fruit cocktail, juice and all, into a well-greased oblong cake pan. Spoon prepared cake mix over this. Melt oleo and pour over mix. Cook at 350 degrees for one hour, or until brown.

QUICK FRUIT COBBLER

1 cup white sugar
1¼ cups self-raising flour
1 cup oleo (two sticks)

1 quart of sliced fruit (your choice)

Blend (with a spoon) oleo and flour. Sprinkle the three ingredients (well mixed) over the fruit, which has been placed in a baking dish. Bake at 350 degrees for 35 minutes or until the top of it is brown.

Ora May Stringer says: "It don't look or sound like much, but you gotta taste it one time and you'll be hooked."

MIZ BILL'S BUCKET DUMPLING

1 pint of flour
2 eggs
2 level teaspoons Calumet
   baking powder
1 quart sweetened
   blackberries

1 large tablespoon oleo
1 large tablespoon Crisco
⅔ cup sweet milk

Mix oleo, Crisco, flour and baking powder. Add eggs, slightly beaten, then milk. Put in a lard can, or mold, and smear around sides. Place one quart of berries in center. Cover mold, or can, and steam in boiling water for three hours. Serve with hard whiskey sauce. This dumpling is more delicious than if you make 'em with Bisquick. If berries are sour, you may add a little sugar. Any other fruit in season, such as apples, peaches, or huckleberries, may be substituted for blackberries.

Serve with canned cream over the top of it. "You won't believe the color," Miz Bill said.

This is like a steam puddin.

POST OFFICE COOKIES

1⅓ sticks oleo
2 cups brown sugar
1 cup flour (measure
   before sifting)
1 cup chopped nuts

1 teaspoon McCormick's
   vanilla extract
pinch salt
2 eggs, beaten together

Cream oleo and sugar; add eggs and flour, vanilla and nuts. Cook in biscuit pan in a slow oven (250 degrees) about 40 minutes. When cold, cut in small pieces and roll in confectioner's powdered sugar.

RUSSIAN COMMUNIST TEA CAKES

1 cup butter
1 cup powdered sugar
2 teaspoons vanilla

dash salt
2 ½ cups flour
½ – 1 cup chopped nuts

Cream butter, sugar, vanilla and salt; then stir in flour and nuts.
Roll into balls, place on sheet. Bake at 350 degrees for 12 – 15 minutes. Roll in powdered sugar while warm and, again, when cool.
"If you make a mistake and use 1 cup of flour instead of 2 ½, they'll come out like thin wafers. They'll be just as delicious but won't make enough for Christmas," says Mrs. Ruby Henley of Social Circle, Georgia.

CHEESE ICE-BOX COOKIES

1 cup grated cheese
1 cup flour
1 teaspoon salt
¼ teaspoon cayenne pepper

1 stick of oleo
1 cup of nut meats
  (your choice)

Cream oleo and cheese. Sift flour, salt, pepper; then add to cheese, oleo, and nut meats. Work into two rolls; wrap in wax paper, put in ice box til chilled. Cut into thin slices and place close together on cookie sheet. Bake at 325 degrees for 12 to 15 minutes.

VICKIE'S STICKIES

Make a Plain and Good Biscuit Dough (page 116), and roll out thin. Spread with butter or oleo and cover with brown sugar. On top of this, sprinkle cinnamon. Start from sides and roll it up like a jelly roll. Cut roll into slices about ¼ inch thick. Place in a well-greased pan. Then on top of each slice, put a little brown sugar and cinnamon (this is for those who really like Stickies sticky). Bake in moderate oven (350 degrees) until brown. Remove from pan while hot.
Dough, using 2 cups of flour, gives 24.

BISHOPS-HATS FIG SURPRISE

2 cups of flour
1 cup of grated *sharp*
   cheddar cheese

1 stick of butter

Blend with a fork the flour, cheese and butter until it's orange all over with no outstanding lumps. Add 2 teaspoons of red pepper or cayenne, and 3 tablespoons of cold water, and mix until a nice dough. Roll out like a pie crust on floured board or rag, and cut into 3-inch triangles or squares. In the middle of each piece, place a stewed or canned fig. If they are large, cut them in half. Then fold points to the center over the fig. Dampen the edges with water or milk and pinch together like a bishop's hat. Bake on an ungreased sheet for 20 – 25 minutes, or until golden brown. Serve piping hot with cocktails.

Florence Ann Rich of Frostproof, Florida, says: "You can put anything you want for the surprise, but fig's the best."

Sweet Pones, Puddins 'n Pies

PLAIN OL' POTATO PONE

1 cup milk	2 teaspoons cinnamon
3 medium-size sweet	3 eggs
potatoes	¼ stick of oleo
1 cup of molasses	

First bake your sweet potatoes, or use some left from supper. Take off the skins and mash them up. To the potatoes, add all other ingredients. Mix well and put in an iron skillet and bake at 350 degrees for 25 – 30 minutes. Now this is a real pone. Dig in and make yourself at home — if you ain't, you oughta be.

This is another one of Betty Sue's favorites.

PLAIN SWEET POTATO PONE

4 cups grated raw yams	1 cup brown sugar
2 cups molasses or dark	1 teaspoon cinnamon
corn syrup	1 cup warm milk

Mix ingredients; pour into greased baking dish. Bake in moderate oven until nice crust forms on top (about 45 minutes). Serve hot with unsweetened cream, plain or whipped.

This is a slight variation on the other pone and will taste a little different.

According to Gerald Comisky, pineapple sherbert, sprinkled with instant yams or chocolate Ovaltine, makes an unusual dessert.

FANCY SWEET POTATO PONE

4 cups raw sweet potatoes (grated)	1 cup raisins
1 cup syrup	3 eggs, well-beaten
½ cup sugar	1 teaspoon allspice
1 cup milk	1 teaspoon cinnamon
½ cup butter	½ teaspoon cloves
½ cup chopped nuts	¼ teaspoon salt

Add well beaten eggs, sugar, spices, and nuts to grated sweet potato.

Melt butter in heavy iron frying pan; add potato mixture; Stir all on top of stove until very hot. Cook in same pan in moderate oven for 45 minutes, stirring from bottom several times. Serve with whipped cream.

Raenelle said: 'This is my recipe but Betty Sue added all the extras, so it's hard to tell it's the one I gave her. She's always changin' things.''

"LIKKER PUDDIN" (PONE)

2½ cups sweet milk	¼ stick oleo
3 medium-sized yams	½ cup blanched, slivered almonds
2 cups sugar	
2 teaspoons cinnamon	½ cup whiskey or rum
3 eggs	

Put milk into 2 quart casserole. Grate your yams, adding them to the milk as you grate them to prevent potatoes from turning dark. Beat eggs well and add sugar gradually. Add cinnamon and almonds and bake in a 300 degree oven for two hours. Just before serving, pour the whiskey or rum over the puddin.

YANKEE PUDDIN

4 sweet potatoes grated	2 sticks oleo
¼ cup Karo syrup	1 cup grated coconut
4 eggs, whole	1 cup chopped pecans
1 cup chopped dates	½ cup cooking sherry
¾ cup chopped raisins	⅛ teaspoon cinnamon and
2 cups sweet milk	allspice
2 cups sugar	

Beat eggs and sugar, fold in all other ingredients and bake for 1 ½ hours at 300 degrees. (A thick casserole dish is best.) This may be served as a dessert, topped with Reddi Whip, but it goes good with meat and vegetables too.

BAKED INDIAN PUDDIN

Place one pint of milk in a stew pan and heat, but do not boil. Into this stir slowly ¼ cup of cornmeal, ¼ cup of molasses and a small piece of oleo. When well mixed, remove from heat and cool.

When cold, add one beaten egg and bake at 350 degrees for about an hour. Serve with Reddi Whip.

CHARLOTTE'S MOTHER'S CHARLOTTE

1 quart heavy cream, beaten very stiff	1 rounded tablespoon unflavored gelatin (in
3 eggs, yolks and whites beaten stiffly, separately	cold weather); use 1 ½ tablespoons if weather is moderate

Soak gelatin in cold water (enough to cover) and let set over kettle of boiling water until it dissolves perfectly. Beat the yolks lightly with one cup of sugar; then add gelatin. Mix rapidly to avoid congealing. Add cream. After mixing, fold in the well-beaten whites and flavor to taste with McCormick's vanilla extract.

GOLDIE'S YO-YO PUDDIN

1 stick oleo margarine (¼ pound)	1 cup white sugar
2 egg yolks	1 small can pineapple
1 cup nut meats (your choice)	2 small boxes Nabsico vanilla wafers

Cream the oleo, sugar, and egg yolks together and add your Nabisco vanilla wafers, pineapple, and nuts. Beat egg whites stiff. Serve topped with Cool Whip.

SKEETER'S CORN PUDDIN

2 cups fresh or canned corn	4 whole eggs
2 tablespoons flour	2 tablespoons white sugar
1 teaspoon salt	1¾ cups sweet milk
6 tablespoons oleo margarine	

Blend oleo, sugar, flour and salt. Add whole eggs, beating well. Stir in corn and milk. Pour ingredients into buttered casserole and bake for 45 minutes at 325 degrees. Only stir once during baking, just when it starts to bubble and just before it sets. When done, puddin will be golden brown and will look and feel just like custard.

SWEET TATER SURPRISE

2 cups warm mashed sweet taters	1 whole egg, beaten
2 tablespoons white sugar	½ teaspoon salt
1 cup crunchy peanut butter	½ cup crushed cornflakes

Combine warm taters with beaten egg, sugar, and salt. Form into balls with peanut butter inside each one. Roll in crushed cornflakes. Brown in oven at 375 degrees. Marshmallows can be used inside the balls with the peanut butter for a little extra treat.

BONNIE JEAN BUTT'S BANANA PUDDIN

6 real ripe bananas	1 large can of crushed
1 box Nabisco vanilla	pineapple
wafers	
2 boxes Royal vanilla	
puddin (the kind you	
cook)	

Put a layer of vanilla wafers in the bottom of a flat glass dish; add a layer of banana slices. Then prepare one of the boxes of puddin and pour it on the layers. Add another layer of wafers and bananas and this time put ½ of the pineapple on top of the bananas. Now add your other box of puddin (prepared) and one more layer of wafers, bananas, and top this with the rest of the pineapple plus the juice. Let it sit until it's cool but not cold. Eat at room temperature for best flavor. It's enough for a picnic.

And Bonnie Jean always said: "No picnic is a picnic less'n you have a banana puddin."

WATER LILY PIE

3 eggs, separated	½ teaspoon almond extract
1 cup sugar	½ teaspoon vanilla
¼ lb. butter	⅛ teaspoon cream of tartar

Beat yolks of three eggs until light, adding, gradually, ½ cup sugar. Cream butter, almond extract and vanilla. Stir this into egg mixture.

Beat egg whites very stiff. Add slowly ½ cup sugar and cream of tartar.

Spread whites over buttered-and-floured pie plate. Push toward edge, making depression in center. Pour filling into middle, very carefully.

Bake in a slow oven nearly an hour.

"It should look just like a water lily — if it don't, you did something wrong," remarks Grace Agnes Brooker of Chattahoochee, Fla.

STELLA LEE'S PUNCH PIE

Take an old apple pie (one from the day-old rack at the supermarket) and punch holes all over the top crust after it's baked. Then pour on the rum or brandy, making sure it gets in all the holes. Now that's good enough, but to make it really something, sprinkle on a little sugar (now don't load it down) and set fire to it. That's what you call making it prissy.

Stella told me that she was "the whitiest trash in all of Alabama," let alone Lick Skillet, which is her home.

NEVER-FAIL CHOCOLATE PIE

4 eggs, separated
1 cup sweet milk
6 level tablespoons of Hershey's cocoa
1 tablespoon of McCormick's vanilla extract

½ cup oleo or one stick
1½ cups white sugar
3 tablespoons of flour
a pinch of salt

Beat egg yolks with half the sugar; add melted oleo. Mix other half of sugar with cocoa and flour. Add a little hot water, only enough to dissolve. Put the two mixtures together and mix thoroughly. Add milk and McCormick's vanilla extract. Don't get too upset if the mixture seems thin. Pour into unbaked 9-inch pie shell and bake until firm, about 30 minutes, at 325 degrees. Cool and cover with Reddi Whip.

YELLOW SQUASH PIE

1 cup white sugar	¾ teaspoon salt
1 teaspoon nutmeg	¾ teaspoon ginger
1 cup of steamed yellow	3 eggs
squash, mashed	1 9-inch unbaked pie shell
1 cup of heavy cream	

Add sugar, salt, and spices to squash and mix thoroughly. Beat eggs, add cream, and mix with squash. Pour mixture into unbaked pie shell. Bake in hot oven (450 degrees) for 10 minutes, then reduce temperature to moderate oven (350 degrees), and bake 40 minutes longer or until knife inserted in center of pie comes out clean. This makes a 9-inch pie.

MARIE'S RIVER CAJUN BREAD PUDDIN

First Layer

In a deep pan or bowl that you can bake in put a layer of stale sliced bread (broken up). Sprinkle this with raisins, to choice, ½ can Angel Flake coconut, and dot with pats of butter (one stick).

Second Layer

Just broken bread.

Third Layer

Repeat first layer, but not quite as thick.

In a large bowl mix 2 cups of sugar and 5 beaten eggs with ½ large bottle of butter flavored vanilla. Then add 1 can of Pet milk, 1 cup of water and 1 cup of sweet milk. Pour this over the layers until it's slightly covered. Use milk if you need more liquid. Now pass it through the oven for 15 minutes and take it out. With a knife or a big spoon poke it down until the liquid rises to the top again. Then you put it back in the oven for an hour. Please do not cook dry.

Meringue

Break ten egg whites in a bowl and beat. When stiffening begins put ½ teaspoon baking powder in and beat to final stiff. Add ¾ cup sugar and beat til sugar melts. Put on pudding and pass it back through the oven til it's brown.

"I've served this to some very fancy cooks and they had to have the recipe." E. Mickler.

SODA CRACKER PIE

12 soda crackers, crumbled
1 cup brown sugar
1 teaspoon McCormick's
    vanilla extract

12 dates, chopped
3 egg whites
1 cup nut meats chopped
    (your choice)

Beat egg whites until foamy. Gradually add sugar and beat until the peaks stand up stiff. Combine crackers, dates, and nuts; gently fold into egg whites. Add vanilla extract. Pour into greased 9-inch pie pan. Bake at 350 degrees for 30 minutes, or until brown. Serve topped with Sealtest ice cream or Reddi Whip.

EASY LEMON PIE

1 large can of Pet milk
1 cup sugar
1 can of Eagle brand
    condensed milk

¾ cup Real Lemon lemon
    juice

Chill the Pet milk thoroughly, then whip. Add condensed milk and sugar. At last, add Real Lemon lemon juice. Pour into Sue Ella Lightfoot's Graham cracker crust (page 111), and chill. Makes two 9-inch pies.

RETHA'S RITZ PIE

23 Ritz crackers
1 cup white sugar
1 teaspoon McCormick's
    vanilla extract

3 egg whites
1 cup chopped pecans

Beat egg whites until stiff. Slowly add sugar and vanilla extract. Crush your Ritz crackers very fine and fold them into egg whites; add pecans. Put into greased pie pan and bake 30 minutes at 350 degrees.

Top with the following whipped together: ½ pint whipping cream, 3 tablespoons of Nestle's instant cocoa, and sugar to taste. Put pie into ice box.

Retha Faye says: "One more cracker and you'd ruin the whole thing!"

BUTTERMILK-SKY PIE

1½ cups of white sugar
2 eggs
1 cup thick buttermilk
1 teaspoon of Real Lemon
    lemon juice
3 tablespoons of flour

½ cup oleo
2 teaspoons McCormick's
    vanilla extract
1 9-inch, chilled, unbaked
    pie shell

Beat your eggs thoroughly and add to your sugar and flour. Add ½ cup oleo, melted, and one cup thick buttermilk. Mix well. Fold in 2 teaspoons McCormick's vanilla extract and 1 teaspoon of Real Lemon lemon juice. Pour into chilled, 9-inch unbaked pie shell. Pre-heat oven and reduce temperature to 350 degrees, and bake 35 minutes without opening the door.

PLUMP'S PUN'KIN PIE

1 cup stewed pumpkin (fresh or canned)	¼ teaspoon salt
1 cup brown sugar	2 cups milk
1 teaspoon ground ginger	2 tablespoons melted oleo
1 teaspoon ground cinnamon	2 eggs

Add sugar and seasonings to the pumpkin and mix well. Add slightly beaten eggs and milk. Lastly, stir in melted oleo. Turn into pie plate lined with pastry and bake in hot oven (425 degrees) for 5 minutes. Lower heat to moderate 350 degrees, and bake until filling is set. A knife inserted in center will come out clean when it's done.

BESSIE'S SWEET POTATO PIE

3 large sweet potatoes	½ teaspoon nutmeg
2 tablespoons oleo	1 egg
½ cup sugar	2 egg whites
½ teaspoon cinnamon	4 teaspoons sugar

Boil potatoes soft. Peel and mash well with 2 tablespoons oleo. Add sugar, cinnamon, nutmeg and egg, well beaten. Fill cooked pastry shell, and cover with meringue made of beaten egg whites and 4 teaspoons of sugar. Brown in medium oven.

PRUNELLA'S PECAN PIE

⅔ cup brown sugar
⅓ cup white corn syrup
2 tablespoons milk
1 heaping tablespoon
   cornmeal
1 egg

1 pinch salt
1 teaspoon McCormick's
   vanilla extract
1 cup pecan meat
1 lump of oleo the size
   of an egg

Mix in order listed; pour into pie pan lined with pastry. Bake in 375-degree oven for 25 minutes.

MOCK PECAN PIE

1 cup Post grapenuts cereal
1 cup light brown sugar,
   firmly packed
¼ cup melted oleo
3 eggs, beaten
1 9-inch unbaked pie shell

¾ cup lukewarm water
1 cup dark Karo corn syrup
1 teaspoon of McCormick's
   vanilla extract
a pinch of salt

Soak Post grapenuts in water until water is absorbed. Combine sugar, Karo syrup, oleo, and salt in saucepan. Bring to boil, stirring until sugar is dissolved. Remove from heat, beat eggs until foamy. Add small amount of hot syrup mixture to eggs. Mix well and add rest of syrup and other ingredients. Bake at 375 degrees for 40 to 50 minutes. You can hardly tell it from the real thing.

Jenny Pansy, of Neck, Florida, says: "We use ta stir up somethin from nothin. Now, they gotta have too much before they begin."

IMOGENE'S IMPOSSIBLE PIE

2 cups milk
½ cup Bisquick
½ stick butter

4 eggs
1 teaspoon vanilla
1¼ cups sugar

Put all into blender in order listed. Blend for 3 minutes. Then, add 1 cup coconut and flash blend. Pour into greased pie pan and bake 45 minutes in a 350-degree oven, or until firm. Check by putting a knife into center. If it comes out clean, pie is done.

CLARA JANE'S UNFORGETTABLE PEACH PIE CRUST

Forget it. No one left alive can make a pie crust like this, so you might as well go buy one, or use Oleta Brown's on page 111.
And now for the filling:

CLARA JANE'S UNFORGETTABLE PEACH PIE

4 medium-size, peeled-
and-sliced, real-ripe
peaches or 1 medium
can, drained
½ teaspoon pure almond
extract
½ teaspoon pure vanilla
extract

½ teaspoon mace
1 cup brown sugar
2 teaspoons of cornstarch
(dissolved in 2
tablespoons of water)

Mix the peaches with everything else. Pour into the best pie shell you can buy or make, and bake in a pre-heated oven at 350 degrees for 30 minutes. And pray to God it turns out like hers!

Remember, Clara Jane used Watkins' pure vanilla extract, Watkins' pure almond essence, and mace only. She combed her hair with a Watkins comb and read her Bible three times a day. This may have been the secret of the pie.

CLARA JANE'S FRIED APPLES

Core 5 apples, slice thin, put in skillet with 2 tablespoons butter or oleo. Cover and cook over low heat for 15 minutes. Eat with ham or pork chops, or serve with canned cream for dessert.

OLETA BROWN'S PIE CRUST

1 cup all-purpose flour	1 tablespoon cold water
1 stick of butter	1 pinch of salt

With a fork or pastry blender, blend butter and flour until thoroughly mixed together with no lumps of butter left. Spoon in water and blend some more with fork. When water is mixed with flour and butter, take it in your hands and knead it soft 3 or 4 times, *no more*. Then, pinch in half and roll out on a floured board or cloth. This makes 2 very thin pie crusts. One for the bottom and one for the top; or, two bottoms.

Aunt Oleta always said you can't make good pie crusts unless you got cold hands, but ice water will help.

SUE ELLA LIGHTFOOT'S GRAHAM CRACKER CRUST

Mash up some Graham crackers with a fork. Mix with oleo margarine until all stuck together. Press into a pie pan. That's all there is to it.

LADY GODIVA PECAN PIE

1 9-inch, frozen pie crust
   (for God's sake, don't
   tell Oleta Brown)
2 oz. Godiva chocolate
2 tablespoons butter

3 eggs
⅓ cup sugar
¾ cup dark molasses
¾ cup pecan halves

Melt chocolate and butter in a double-boiler, or anything you can rig up. Cool it down. Then, heat eggs, sugar, chocolate mixture, and molasses together. Stir in pecans. Put in the pie shell and bake for 40 – 50 minutes at 375 degrees, or until it sets.

FLORENCE'S PIE CRUST

3 cups flour
1 teaspoon salt
1¼ cups lard or Cresco
1 beaten egg

1 tablespoon sugar
1 teaspoon vinegar
5 tablespoons cold water

Combine flour and salt, cut in lard, or shortening; add eggs, water, and vinegar. Moisten dry ingredients; work with fingers; roll out and place on pie plate. Bake at 350 degrees.

This crust is so thick you'll be ashamed of it.

FLORENCE'S LEMON ICE-BOX PIE

1 can frozen lemonade
1 can condensed milk

1 large container Cool
   Whip

Mix all together and pour it in your pie shell. Then refrigerate, before serving à la Florence.

Cornpones,
Cornbreads,
Biscuits 'n Rolls

BIG MAMMA'S CRACKLIN CORN PONE

Cracklins are the skins and other pieces left after the rendering of pork fat at hog-killing time (in the Fall after the first cold snap). Pig skins are a passable substitute.

1 cup milk (boiling)	⅔ cup cracklins, or 1 cup
2 cups cornmeal	of pig skins
1 teaspoon baking powder	2 tablespoons bacon
½ teaspoon salt	drippins

Sift your cornmeal, baking soda, and salt into a bowl. Then, pour enough boiling milk into this to make a good and stiff batter. Add the cracklins, or pig skins, and bacon drippins. Pour in a black skillet and bake at 425 degrees until golden. Make sure the skillet is well greased.

Some people shape into pones (small oval shapes) and bake.

Mavis Drew, of Improve, Mississippi, says: "If someone's eatin corn pone for the first time, this is the one that'll make a believer out of 'em!"

COMMON CORN PONE

2 cups cornmeal	1 teaspoon salt
½ teaspoon baking soda	1 tablespoon bacon
1 egg	drippins
½ cup of molasses (cane)	

Add enough warm water to the cornmeal to make a thin dough. Put it in a warm place (the oven) and let it sit and rise overnight. When you are ready to use, add everything else, mix well, and bake in a skillet at 400 degrees until golden. Slice and eat.

You can make one big pone in the middle of the skillet, if you want to.

FRESH-FRIED CORN PONE

1 cup cornmeal	½ teaspoon salt
1 tablespoon drippins	1 teaspoon molasses

Mix everything together, and pour enough hot water over it to make a batter that runs but does not pour. Spoon into hot greased skillet and fry like you would pancakes. Serve with black-eyed peas and greens.

PLAIN AND GOOD BISCUITS

2 cups flour	4 tablespoons of shortening
3 – 4 pinches of salt	(hog lard is best)
1 tablespoon of baking	1 cup of milk (sweet or
powder	evaporated)

Sift everything except the shortening and milk. Then, with a fork, cut the shortening into the flour until it's all blended and is like a bunch of crumbs. Make a big hole in the flour and pour in all the milk at once, stirring until everything is blended real good. Then dump the mixture onto a floured table or cloth and knead it for a little while, but not too long. Roll it out with a floured rolling pin to about ½-inch thick, and cut with a jelly glass. Place on a cookie sheet and bake at 450 degrees for 12 to 15 minutes.

Another way: After the dough is kneaded, with all four fingers and your thumb pinch off enough to almost cover the palm of your well-floured hand. With the other hand, roll it into a ball gently. Then, pat it until it's about ½-inch thick. Place on a cookie sheet, and put the imprint of the back of your fingers on the top of each biscuit.* Repeat until all the dough is used and bake at 450 degrees for 12 – 15 minutes.

* *"Back home I didn't know I was eating biscuits unless I saw the fingerprints on top."* — E. Mickler.

DUMPLINS OR DROP BISCUITS

2 cups flour (all-purpose)
3 tablespoons Calumet
   baking powder
1 teaspoon salt

⅓ cup oil (lard or
   vegetable)
⅔ cup plain milk

Heat oven to 450 degrees. Mix flour, baking powder and salt together with a fork. Then add all at once oil and milk.

Stir with your fork until it makes a ball in the bowl. For biscuits, spoon-drop them on a greased baking sheet, and bake for 10 – 14 minutes.

For dumplins, spoon-drop them into a boiling stew of meat, vegetables, or fruit. Cook them for 15 – 20 minutes, turning them one by one.

SODA WATER PANCAKES

1½ cups all-purpose flour
1 teaspoon salt
1 tablespoon of sugar
1 egg (beaten)

3 tablespoons shortening
¼ cup club soda
1 cup of milk

Sift flour by itself and then do it one more time with salt and sugar. Mix this with other ingredients. When mixture is smooth, spoon the batter on to a very hot griddle or cast iron skillet that has been rubbed with cooking oil. Make them small or large, but turn them only once (after 3 – 4 minutes) and brown the other side. For the real thing, serve with cane syrup and butter and hot sausage.

If you cook a pile of them, place them in a 200-degree oven separated by paper towels. They stay warm and moist.

UNCLE CHARLIE'S CORNBREAD (REGULAR)

1 pint cornmeal (pure)
1 teaspoon of salt
¾ pint of buttermilk or
    plain milk

¾ teaspoon soda
1 egg
1 large spoon of shortening
    or bacon grease

Mix cornmeal with milk, eggs, salt, and dissolved soda. Then, add melted shortening to mixture. Pour it all in a well-greased black iron skillet and bake in a hot oven til golden brown. About 350-400 degrees for 35-40 minutes.

If you want cracklin bread, add a fistful of cracklins. It's almost as good as Big Mamma's (page 115).

"Now, if you want a cornbread that's extra crusty, just heat your well-greased skillet on top of the stove until it's sizzlin' hot. Then pour in the batter and pop it in the oven. Just make sure you remember that this cuts down on the baking time by ten minutes or more." — *Uncle Charlie.*

CORNBREAD IN A GLASS

Pour buttermilk in a big ice-tea glass filled with toasted cornbread. Let the bread soak up the buttermilk and then eat it with a long ice-tea spoon.

Also good with sweet milk and soda crackers.

HANNAH'S HOE CAKES (HARD-HEARTED)

Pour enough very hot (not boiling) milk or water on some salted cornmeal. Just enough to make it soupy but not runny. Then, let it sit for an hour or longer. You can then put 2 or 3 teaspoons of this on a hot greased griddle or black iron frying pan. Pat it down smooth to make a cake about ½-inch thick. Lightly brown one side, then the other, and serve piping hot with beans, greens, or whatever you got.

You can also cook these on the blade of a hoe on an open fire. That's how they got their name.

JOHNNYBOY'S CORN CORNBREAD

1 cup fresh corn (cut from
    the cob) or 1 cup of
    whole kernel corn from
    can (drained)
1 egg
1 tablespoon sugar
2 tablespoons oil

½ medium size onion
    (chopped)
1½ cups cornmeal
½ cup flour
    milk (enough to make it
    like pancake batter)
salt and pepper

Fresh corn must be fried in a little bit of oil for 6 minutes on medium heat. (Remember, canned corn must be drained).

In a medium size bowl, mix cornmeal, flour, eggs, milk, sugar, salt, pepper, corn and onion.

Pour mixture into greased baking pan and bake at 350 degrees for 35 or 40 minutes or until top starts to brown slightly. Remove from oven and slice in squares and serve piping hot with butter. Serves 4 – 6.

SPOON BREAD

1 cup yellow cornmeal
2½ teaspoons Calumet
    baking powder

2 eggs, separated
1½ teaspoons salt
2 cups of scalded milk

Mix cornmeal and salt. Add hot milk, and cook in double-boiler until thick and smooth, stirring it once in a while. Take it off the stove and cool it. Pour in well-beaten egg yolks, and fold in stiffly-beaten egg whites. Place in greased casserole, which has also had one tablespoon of melted fat. Bake in moderate oven, 375 degrees, for 35 minutes, or until firm and the crust is brown. Very rich and filling.

CORN BREAD MUFFINS

1 cup cornmeal	1 teaspoon Calumet baking
1 cup bread flour	powder
2 tablespoons sugar	2 tablespoons melted oleo
1¼ cups milk	2 well-beaten eggs
1 teaspoon salt	

Sift dry ingredients. Beat (in a separate bowl) milk, oleo, and eggs. Add to dry ingredients. Beat lightly, until thoroughly mixed. Then, partly fill hot muffin tins and bake in quick oven, 450 degrees, for 15 to 20 minutes.

THREE-HOUR SUNDAY ROLLS

2 packages of yeast	2 cups lukewarm water
2 whole eggs	½ cup white sugar
½ cup Wesson oil	1 teaspoon of salt

Add enough plain flour to make a thick batter. Set for one hour. Make into rolls and let 'em set for one more hour to rise. Grease top of rolls with oleo. Bake at 500 degrees. It takes about 15 minutes to bake and brown and serve.

HUSH PUPPIES

2 cups cornmeal	1 tablespoon Calumet
1 teaspoon soda	baking powder
1 teaspoon salt	1 egg
6 tablespoons chopped	2 cups buttermilk
onion	red pepper to taste
2 tablespoons flour	

Mix all dry ingredients; add chopped onion, then milk and egg, beaten together. Drop by small spoonfuls into frying pan with ½-inch hot grease. Brown one side; turn and brown the other.

If you throw these to the dogs, it'll hush 'em up. That's how they got their names.

For coastal hush puppies, throw in 3 – 4 tablespoons chopped bell pepper.

Pickles 'n Jellies

ICED TOMATO PICKLES

3 lbs. sugar	1 teaspoon allspice
2 pints vinegar	1 teaspoon celery seed
1 teaspoon cloves	1 teaspoon mace
1 teaspoon ginger	1 teaspoon cinnamon

Slice 7 pounds of green tomatoes, and soak in lime water for 24 hours. (Use three cups lime to 2 gallons water.) Drain. Soak in fresh water for 4 hours, changing water every hour. Drain.

Then make syrup of above ingredients. Bring to boil and pour over tomatoes. Let stand overnight. Next morning, boil one hour, and seal while hot.

These are crispy pickles.

BREAD & BUTTER PICKLES

1 quart sliced cucumbers	1 teaspoon salt
1 large onion, sliced	¼ teaspoon dry mustard
¾ cup sugar	¼ teaspoon turmeric
¾ cup vinegar (white)	1 teaspoon mustard seeds

Wash and slice cucumbers. Place cucumbers and onions in a large pot with everything else. Bring to a boil, stirring occasionally. Pour into sterilized jars, making certain liquid covers cucumbers. Seal. They are ready to eat in 2 or 3 days. Cold.

Mrs. Lynnwood Dyal says: "This is the real ole country pickle that taste so good in a sandwich."

PEAR SQUASH PICKLES (CHAYOTES)

6 chayotes (average size)
3 white onions, cut into
   rings
3 4-inch slices of celery
   (per jar)
1 quart vinegar (cider)

1 ½ cups sugar
¼ cup salt
1 teaspoon mustard seed
1 teaspoon turmeric
3 toes of garlic (per jar)

Peel chayotes, and slice lengthwise ¼-inch thick. Then, soak onions, celery, and chayotes for 5 hours in ice water. Boil vinegar, salt, and sugar. Set aside. Pack chayotes, onions, celery, and garlic into jars, along with hot pepper, mustard seed, and turmeric. (Divide evenly.) Pour boiling-hot mixture over pickles, and seal. Process ten minutes. Do not boil.

AUNT WILL'S PLUM JELLY

4 cups plum juice
6 ½ cups sugar

½ bottle Certo

Place on high heat and bring to boil, stirring constantly. Add Certo and bring to *rolling* boil for one minute. Remove. Skim foam. Pour in jars and seal.

    Aunt Will always said: "Never throw anything away. You never know when you're going to need it. Remind yourself of this before you throw away those mayonnaise jars and jelly glasses."

GERALDINE'S GREEN PEPPER JELLY

2 cups ground bell peppers
7½ cups white sugar
1½ cups Heinz white vinegar

1 bottle liquid fruit pectin
few drops green food
coloring

Boil peppers, sugar, and vinegar together for 6 minutes. Add the liquid pectin and boil for 3 minutes. Add 2 or 3 drops food coloring, if desired. Pour into sterilized jars. Cover with parafin, and store. Makes about a dozen half-pint jars.

AUNT ADA'S ORANGE MARMALADE

8 oranges: squeeze juice; grind pulp and rind; add juice. Add 1 cup of water for each cup of orange mixture (juice and rind).

Boil 10 minutes.

Add 1 can (large) crushed pineapple and boil 10 minutes longer. Let it stand overnight or 12 hours. Measure again: 1 cup mixture to 1½ cups sugar. Boil and stir until thick. Just before taking off the fire, add 1 bottle maraschino cherries and nuts, if desired.

Put in sterilized jars and cover with parafin.

Aunt Ada made this orange marmalade every Christmas. She'd put it in a palmetto hat she'd made and give it away as a present.

Drinks

ICE TEA SOUTH

In a saucepan of boiling water drop 5 or 6 tea bags. Turn off the fire and let them stand for ½ hour on the back of the stove. When cool, squeeze tea bags out and throw them away. Pour into an ice-tea pitcher. Finish filling with cold water and sweeten to taste. Pour in a tall glass over ice, add sprig of mint, and serve with a wedge of lemon. Nothin' like it.

For a different treat, cut 2 lemons in slices, add to the pitcher, and let it stand for an hour before serving. Tangy.

In a gallon jar filled with fresh water, put 10 – 12 tea bags. Screw on the lid and let it set in the sun for a whole day. Makes a smooth and mellow tea while you busy yourself with your daily chores.

LOW CALORIE PICK-ME-UP

1 glass skim milk   1 envelope sugar substitute

Blend in blender until foamy, then add 1 teaspoon McCormick's vanilla extract.

Try this on hot days when your cardboard Good-Shepherd fan makes you even hotter.

Betty Sue says: "This is a life-saver before Sunday dinner and just after church, when it's so hot you cain't hardly stand it!"

HIGH CALORIE PICK-ME-UP

Pour a small bag of Tom's peanuts into a cold Pepsi. Turn it up and eat and drink at the same time.

Raenelle told me that this was one of Betty Sue's concoctions. She said: 'But it's so trashy she won't own up to it!"

MARTHA'S HOT COCOA

In a pan, put ½ cup hot water, 1 tablespoon butter, 2 tablespoons cocoa, 2 tablespoons sugar. Boil one minute; add 3 cups of milk; re-heat. Serve with marshmallows and more love. It's better than Bayer.

CHILDREN'S COFFEE

¾ glass milk
¼ glass coffee

3 teaspoons sugar

CAJUN ANISETTE

8 cups sugar

12 cups water

Boil sugar and water. Then turn fire off.
    Add 1 teaspoon oil of anise.
    Color with pink food coloring and when cold, add a fifth of vodka.
    Let stand six weeks before using, and you can't tell it from bought.

COFFEE PUNCH

1 gallon strong coffee
1 quart cream
5 tablespoons white sugar
2 quarts of Sealtest vanilla
    ice cream

5 teaspoons McCormick's
    vanilla extract

Chill coffee. Whip cream, add sugar and vanilla. Place ice cream and whipped cream in punch bowl and pour your coffee over it. Mix well before serving.

AFTER-DINNER COFFEE LIQUEUR

  8 cups sugar
12 cups double-strength
      coffee (instant will do)

Heat the coffee with sugar in it and stir until all sugar has disappeared. (Check the bottom.) Add one fifth of vodka and a tablespoon of vanilla extract.

It's better if you let it set for six weeks before you drink it.

BLACKBERRY ACID

1 gallon blackberries,   sugar
   unwashed
1 oz. tartaric acid

Put berries in stone crock, cover with water and add acid. Let stand for 24 hours, then strain. To each pint of liquid add a pound of sugar. Boil for 20 minutes. Bottle hot, and keep in a dry, cool place. Serve ice cold, diluted with water, or else over crushed ice. If you're lucky, it'll ferment.

STRAWBERRY PUNCH

   1 package strawberry   1 can orange juice, frozen
      Kool-Aid   1 flat can crushed
   1 gallon water   pineapple
2½ cups sugar   1 box frozen, sliced
   2 cans lemonade, frozen   strawberries

Mix, sweeten to taste. Add red food coloring if desired. Makes about two gallons. Part may be frozen as ice cubes, or an ice ring, to cool punch without diluting it.

MIAMI PUNCH

3 No. 2 cans orange or   1 quart ginger ale,
   tangerine juice, chilled   chilled
2 pints pre-packaged
   vanilla ice cream

Pour chilled orange or tangerine juice and ginger ale into punch bowl; mix well. Drop ice cream by the heaping tablespoons into mixture. Stir until ice cream is partially melted. In Miami that won't take long.

WHITE TRASH NOTES

WHITE TRASH NOTES

WHITE TRASH NOTES

WHITE TRASH NOTES

WHITE TRASH NOTES

ABOUT THE AUTHOR

I was born in Palm Valley, Florida. It's a cabbage-palm swamp, near St. Augustine, split wide open by the Inland Coastal Waterway. From there, Alberta West drove the school bus twenty-five miles every day. A snob named Russell Bryant printed in the high-school yearbook, "Ernie Mickler lives in the sticks with all the rest of the Palm Valley hicks." I hated school after that and was glad to graduate.

Petie Pickette and I became a duo, writing and singing country music. She's the granddaughter of Tutti's Fruited Porkettes. And we sang with the best: Skeeter Davis, Maybelle Carter, Faron Young, Roy Orbison and Patsy Cline. After two years and three records, we got tired and quit.

Petie bought a shiny black Ford and got a job selling Avon products. I moved to the ocean and started making birds from driftwood and shells. Memphis Wood, Art Director of Jacksonville University, found me and directed me through a Bachelor of Fine Arts Degree. Shortly thereafter, I upped and moved to California. Again with the help of Memphis, I talked my way into Mills College. And walked out of Mills with a Master of Fine Arts and started this book.

Away I went, down every back road between Slap Out and Slap In. But in Mexico the sacks and boxes started looking like a book. Finally, at the very end of U.S.1 I found Key West, a bastion of White Trash, eagerly awaiting my born-again cuisine. In this southernmost spot, I met all of the people that knew what to do to get my cookbook into print.

WHITE TRASH COOKING: it's a dream come true. I can just hear Raenelle and Betty Sue at every Tupperware party in Rolling Fork saying, "Ernie went from white trash to WHITE TRASH overnight."

Ernest Matthew Mickler
Key West, Florida
1985